COLLINS HISTORY CONNECTIONS 2

The Making of the United Kingdom 1500–1750

The French Revolution and Napoleon

Christopher Culpin
Fiona Macdonald

Collins
Educational

An Imprint of
HarperCollins*Publishers*

Contents

The Making of the United Kingdom — 6

UNIT 1 The new monarchy — 8

UNIT 2 People and homes — 20

UNIT 3 Kings and Parliaments — 32

UNIT 4 Searching for a settlement — 46

The French Revolution and Napoleon — 62

UNIT 5 Land and people — 64

UNIT 6 The Revolution — 76

UNIT 7 Napoleon — 96

UNIT 8 A new Europe — 116

Glossary — 123

Index — 126

---

attainment target

This symbol appears with questions targeted at the attainment target for history. At the end of Year 9 you will be given a level in history on the basis of how well you have answered these questions.

Some questions are about how much you know about different periods in the past: how people lived and what they believed. Others are about how things change through history and why these changes happen.

People are always trying to describe the past and sometimes they say different things. You will be asked about these differences and why they occur.

We find out about the past from historical sources. You will be asked about how we can use these sources to reach conclusions about the past.

Introduction

History does not repeat itself. Sometimes, however, things happen which seem strikingly similar. There are two stories in this book. One, in Britain, starts with the story you may remember from your primary school of the strong Tudor kings and queens. In the 17th century, the kings got into conflict with parliament which wanted more say in how the country was run. There was a civil war, the king lost, and was executed. An army general called Oliver Cromwell seized power and ran the country. After his death the monarchy was restored.

The other story, in 18th-century France, starts with equally powerful French kings. They got into conflict with the Estates-General, which wanted more say in how the country was run. The king was executed and France was invaded. Then Napoleon, an army general, ran the country. When Napoleon died the monarchy was restored.

As you follow these separate stories, look for similarities and differences between events in Britain and France. At various points in the book you will find 'Making Connections' pages to help you do this.

MAKING CONNECTIONS

Changes and revolutions

All around you things are changing, sometimes slowly, sometimes quickly. Fashions in clothes and music, for example: what is fashionable one year can look (or sound) very dated the next. But most changes, however rapid they seem, are planned and controlled. They don't cause major upheavals, death and bloodshed or significant changes to people's lives.

Other changes are different. They are sudden, unexpected and, perhaps, violent. The pace of change may be out of control. People's lives are altered dramatically, and for ever. We often call this kind of political change a revolution.

What makes a revolution?

All revolutions aim to overthrow an existing government. Often, the old government leaders are executed or exiled. But not all revolutions have the same ambitions. For example, the Russian revolution of 1917 (Source 1) aimed to introduce a communist government, while the Romanian revolution of 1989 (Source 2) hoped to remove a communist dictator.

Revolutions are not all caused by the same factors, either. They may result from crisis situations, such as famine or military defeat. Or they may be the result of long-term hardships that finally 'explode' in mass protests and demonstrations. Some revolutions are plotted by small groups of conspirators; others happen when mobs of ordinary people riot and seize power.

'Real' revolutions?

Originally, the word revolution was used to describe political changes only (see Source 3). Then the phrase 'industrial revolution' (Source 4) was coined to describe a variety of gradual, long-term changes: economic, social and technological. More recently, the word 'revolution' has been used in a variety of situations: describing astonishing advances in technology (Source 5) and even for marketing new products (Source 6).

In this book, you will find out about events in 17th century England and 18th century France. As you read, try to think about whether they were revolutions or not.

SOURCE 1
In Russia in 1917 crowds forced the country's ruler, Tsar Nicholas II, to quit and a new system of government was set up. Old noble titles, like duke, were abolished and the state took over factories, businesses and large estates. Many people were killed.

SOURCE 2
Romania in 1989: crowds forced President Ceaucescu, who had ruled the country on his own since 1974, to quit. Many of his special police were killed. A new democratic government was set up.

MAKING CONNECTIONS

Look at Sources 1 to 6 which show episodes from the recent past or from history. Discuss the sources in groups. Are they all revolutions? To decide, you should think about the following questions:
a was the change rapid?
b were lots of people affected?
c was it a violent change?
d did it change things forever?

SOURCE 3
Crowds demonstrating peacefully in East Germany in 1989 led the government to quit. East Germany had been a separate country since 1945 but in 1989 a new democratic government was set up and East Germany was unified with West Germany to form one nation.

SOURCE 4
A 19th century view of Manchester. In 1750 most people in Britain lived in the countryside and worked on the land or made things in their own homes. The fastest anyone could travel was at the speed of a galloping horse. In 1850 (about the time when this engraving was made) the majority of people lived in towns or cities, many goods were made in factories and you could travel by train at 40 miles per hour (65 kilometres per hour).

SOURCE 5
Over the last ten years developments in technology have brought enormous changes to our daily lives. Televisions, telephones and computers have all become more advanced and we rely on them for education, office work, healthcare, shopping, banking and entertainment.

SOURCE 6
This advertisement for a personal stereo carried the slogan 'First, the Walkman sensation. Now, a Walkman revolution'.

THE MAKING OF THE UK

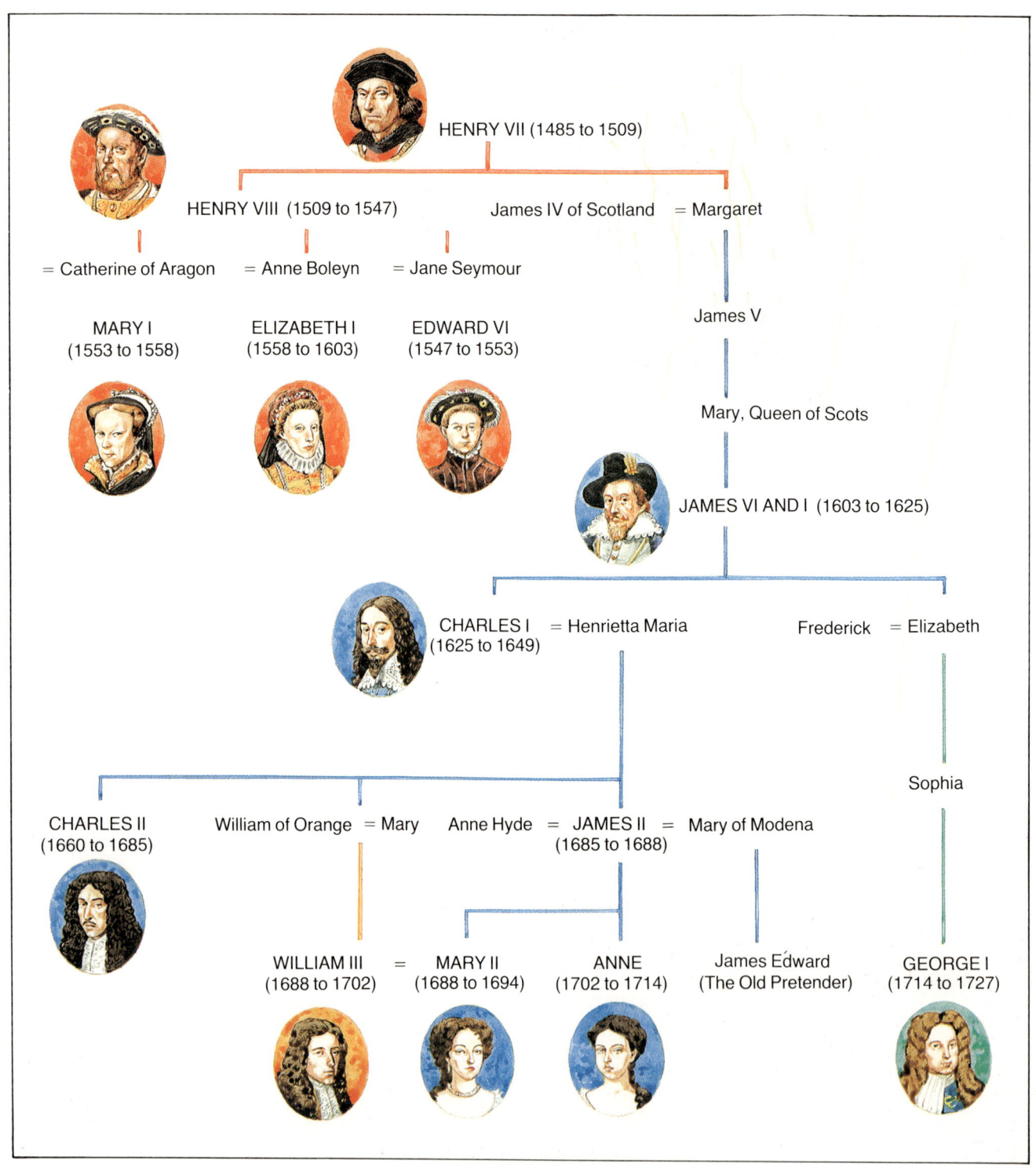

In the family tree of the Tudor and Stuart monarchs above, the Tudor family is shown in red and the Stuart family in blue. Those members who reigned as monarchs are shown in capital letters. The lengths of their reigns and some of the important events in them can be found in the timeline on page 7.

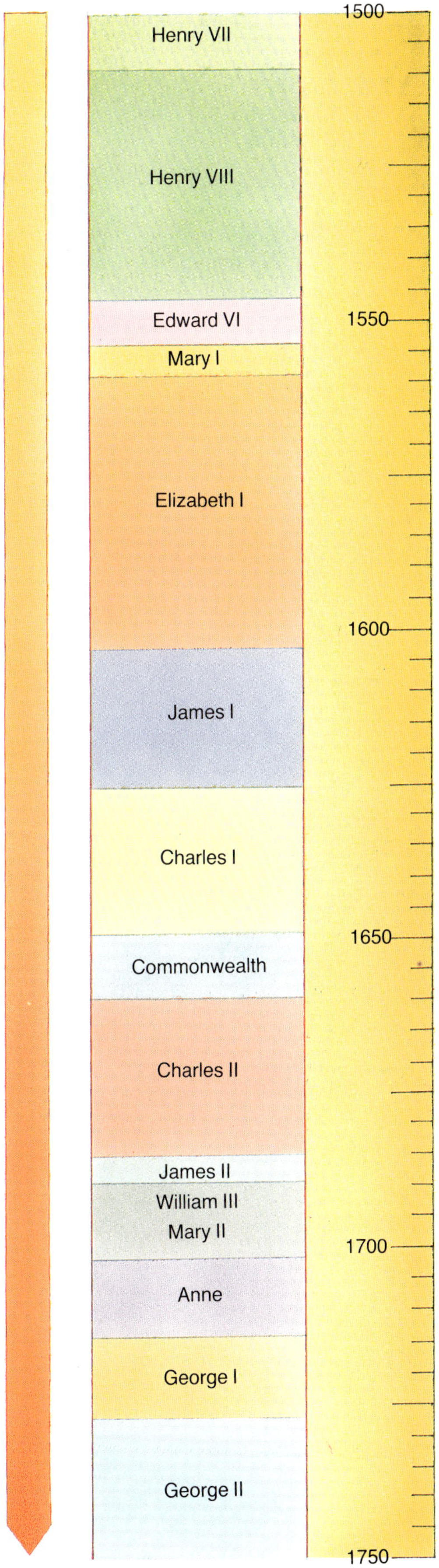

THE MAKING OF THE UK

TIMELINE

1520 Field of the Cloth of Gold

1534 Act of Supremacy
1536 to 1540 Dissolution of the Monasteries
1536 to 1543 Acts of Union with Wales

1588 Bible translated into Welsh

1605 Gunpowder Plot

1620 Pilgrim Fathers go to America
1628 Petition of Right

1638 English Prayer Book introduced into Scotland
1642 Beginning of Civil War
1649 Execution of Charles I

1658 Death of Oliver Cromwell
1662 Royal Society founded
1666 Fire of London

1690 Battle of the Boyne

1707 Act of Union with Scotland

UNIT 1

The new monarchy

AIMS

In this unit we will find out about the reign of King Henry VIII (1509 to 1547). We will see how he increased his power over his kingdom of England and Wales and over the Church.

Henry brought great changes to the religious life of England and Wales. We will go on to see how his three children, all of whom became monarchs, also brought changes in religion. We will look at how far these changes affected the lives of the people.

Henry VIII

When Henry VIII became king in 1509 he was just under 18 years old, nearly 2 metres tall, broad-shouldered and athletic. He loved hunting, as Source 1 explains, but was also excellent at archery, wrestling, tennis, bowls and jousting. Jousting was a medieval sport, still popular in the early 16th century: two knights on horseback, carrying wooden lances, would charge at each other and try to knock the other off his horse. Henry made his jousting partner, Charles Brandon, duke of Suffolk. Like many fit men, Henry became fat when he stopped taking exercise as he grew older. Source 2 shows his jousting armour from later in his life. It is 137 cm round the waist.

These physical skills alone would have made Henry popular in the Middle Ages, but by the 16th century people admired other skills as well. Henry was a good musician and composed songs. He was also a friend of some of the cleverest Englishmen of his time, like John Colet and Thomas More.

'His Majesty is 29 years old and extremely handsome. Nature could not have done more for him. On hearing that Francis I (King of France) wore a beard, he allowed his own to grow and as it is reddish, he now has a beard that looks like gold. He is very talented, a good musician, speaks French, Latin and Spanish, is very religious, attends three services a day when he hunts and sometimes five on other days. He is very fond of hunting and sometimes tires out eight or ten horses in a day.'

SOURCE 1
A description of Henry VIII in 1520 by the Venetian ambassador to London.

SOURCE 2
This suit of armour was made for Henry VIII towards the end of his life.

THE NEW MONARCHY

The power of the ruler

In the later Middle Ages several kings were removed from the throne by powerful barons. Some were killed in battle or ASSASSINATED. Henry VIII's father, Henry VII, had only become king by defeating and killing Richard III at the battle of Bosworth in 1485. Henry VII had to work hard to hold on to the throne, especially in the early years of his reign. Henry VIII was determined to be a powerful and respected king. As we shall see in this unit, he increased the power of the monarchy in several ways. For this reason, he is sometimes called a 'New Monarch'.

One aspect of New Monarchy was that monarchs displayed their wealth and power on every possible occasion. Henry VIII's physical abilities and intelligence helped him to do this. He also rivalled other kings in Europe. Source 3 shows a grand meeting he held in 1520 with King Francis I of France just outside Calais called the Field of the Cloth of Gold. He built a huge temporary palace of timber and canvas. Hundreds of pounds worth of velvet, satin and cloth of gold were shipped across to decorate the tents or for attendants' clothes. Francis did the same, and they promised to be allies, a promise that only lasted 18 months.

1 Make a list of Henry VIII's skills and abilities. Divide your list into 'Physical' and 'Intellectual'.

2 The sources on these pages have been chosen to give a powerful impression of Henry. Do you think he seems to be:
   a a good king?
   b a nice person?

Think about your own judgement of Henry as you read more about him on the next few pages.

SOURCE 3
A painting of the 'Field of the Cloth of Gold' in 1520 showing some of the prefabricated buildings and many richly-hung tents. You can see Henry and Cardinal Wolsey in the bottom left-hand corner.

THE NEW MONARCHY

Henry's rule

Henry found the business of governing the country boring. He was happy to leave it to the able men he chose as his chief MINISTERS. These men became very powerful, but fell into disgrace if they failed to deliver what Henry wanted.

Thomas Wolsey was Henry's first minister and held supreme power from 1515 to 1529. Many were jealous of him, but he governed well, as Source 4 shows.

Peace was not really to Henry's liking. Great kings made their names in war. Wars also kept powerful barons busy. Henry went to war with England's old enemy, France, three times in his reign. Scotland, a separate country at this time, usually joined in on France's side. The English inflicted crushing defeats on the Scots at Flodden in 1513 and Solway Moss in 1547. Henry also took a personal interest in building up the navy (see Source 5).

> And for your realm our Lord be thanked that it never was in such peace and TRANQUILLITY. For all this summer I have heard neither of riot, robbery or burglary, but that your laws be in every place administered without leaning of any matter.

SOURCE 4
Extract from a letter written by Wolsey to Henry VIII.

Henry and the Church

Several medieval monarchs had clashed with the Church because it was outside their control. The Pope in Rome was the head of the Church. Henry was loyal to the Pope. He had no sympathy with the attacks on the Pope by Martin Luther, the German founder of PROTESTANTISM. If you look at any British coin you will see, on the 'heads' side, the letters F.D. (or Fid. Def.). These stand for *Fidei Defensor* (Defender of the Faith), a title given to Henry by the Pope in 1521 for writing a book criticising Luther. In 1525 William Tyndale translated the Bible into English. This was against the law and copies had to be smuggled into the country. Henry had those caught doing this executed.

SOURCE 5
The *Mary Rose*. Launched in 1515, the *Mary Rose* had 207 guns and was designed to carry 1,000 soldiers as well as the crew. She sank suddenly off Portsmouth in 1545 when she turned sharply and water entered the gun-ports. Only 30 people survived drowning.

THE NEW MONARCHY

SOURCE 6
Catherine of Aragon.

SOURCE 7
Anne Boleyn.

By the late 1520s, however, Henry's feelings were changing. In 1509 he had married Catherine of Aragon (Source 6), a Spanish princess who had earlier been briefly married to his elder brother Arthur. Henry loved Catherine in the early years of their marriage. However, they only had one daughter, Mary, and Catherine was now too old to have any more children.

Henry felt he had to have a son to be king when he died and he had fallen in love with Anne Boleyn (Source 7), a much younger woman. He therefore wanted to divorce Catherine and marry Anne. For ROMAN CATHOLICS, to this day, the only person who can grant a divorce is the Pope. Wolsey failed to persuade the Pope to agree. He fell from power and died in 1529. In the same year the Pope came under the influence of the Emperor Charles, Catherine's nephew. Charles did not want his aunt removed as queen.

ACTIVITY

Do this activity in groups of two or three. There are perhaps four possible solutions to Henry's problem, or 'The King's Great Matter' as it was called:

a Decide that Catherine's marriage to Henry is illegal. Henry can therefore marry Anne.
b Persuade Catherine to become a nun. This would end the marriage and Henry could therefore marry Anne. However, Catherine can only do this voluntarily and she has so far refused.
c Find a reason for delay, hoping the situation will change.
d Decide that Catherine's marriage to Henry is legal and so a divorce is impossible.

1 Some groups are advisers to the Pope. Some are members of Henry's Council. Each group chooses one of the four solutions, or makes up another solution of their own, giving their reasons for choosing their solution and rejecting the others. Exchange views in the whole class.

2 What is your opinion of this extraordinary situation from the point of view of a late 20th-century person? Are there different views between the boys and the girls in your class?

> 'Mine own sweetheart, this shall be to tell you of my great loneliness that I find here since your departing. For I assure you the time seems longer since your leaving than the last fortnight. I think your kindness and the strength of my love causes it.'

SOURCE 8
Extract from a letter to Anne written by Henry.

THE NEW MONARCHY

Head of the Church

The job of carrying out what Henry wanted now fell to Thomas Cromwell (Source 9). This clever man made enormous changes to English government and the Church. Most of these changes were carried out through Parliament, so all the leading people in England were involved, and could feel consulted. Working this way also allowed Henry to tell foreigners that it was Parliament that was making these changes, not him. It was Cromwell, however, who managed the Parliament.

Events moved quickly:

- **1532** Parliament made the Church in England agree that Henry was their Head. Anne Boleyn became pregnant.
- **1533** Henry secretly married Anne. Thomas Cranmer became Archbishop of Canterbury and declared that Henry was never legally married to Catherine. Anne Boleyn was crowned Queen.
- **1534** Parliament passed Act of Supremacy, making Henry Supreme Head of the Church in England (see Source 10). Parliament ended payment of taxes to the Pope. Parliament brought in death penalty for anyone refusing to take an oath of loyalty to Henry as Head of the Church.
- **1534** Sir Thomas More (Source 11) was executed for refusing to take the oath.

SOURCE 9
Thomas Cromwell.

'The King's Majesty justly and rightfully is and ought to be the supreme head of the Church in England . . . Yet for confirmation thereof and for increase of Christ's religion in this realm of England, be it enacted by authority of this present Parliament that the King our Sovereign Lord shall be accepted the only Supreme Head of the Church of England.'

SOURCE 10
An extract from the Act of Supremacy, 1534.

SOURCE 11
Thomas More, painted by Holbein.

Discuss your answers to these questions in pairs.

1. How did Thomas Cromwell succeed in solving Henry's problem where Wolsey had failed?
2. What part did Parliament play in these changes?

THE NEW MONARCHY

Dissolution of the Monasteries

Thomas Cromwell also promised to make Henry the richest monarch in Europe. He planned to do this by closing the monasteries and nunneries. There were 513 monasteries and 130 nunneries in England and Wales. Between them they owned about a quarter of the land. Many people criticised the monks and nuns and were jealous of their wealth. Certainly some abbots lived like rich landowners (see Source 13). A few monks and nuns failed to live up to the strict standards they were supposed to keep. But that had always been so and there is no evidence that things were any worse in the 1530s.

However, all monks and nuns were supposed to be loyal to the Pope, not the king. Thomas Cromwell therefore had two ways of attacking them: for refusing to accept Henry as Head of the Church or for misbehaviour.

In 1535 Cromwell sent visitors to all the monasteries and nunneries looking for these things. He also had a valuation made of their wealth: the *Valor Ecclesiasticus* (see Source 14). In 1536 all religious houses worth less than £200 per year were closed by Act of Parliament: 270 were shut down. The larger houses then surrendered gradually, until by 1539 they had all been suppressed. Monks and nuns were given pensions varying from £50 a year for an abbot to £3 a year for a nun. Hardly anyone resisted, but the abbot of Glastonbury Abbey and two of his monks objected and were executed on Glastonbury Tor. Henry was richer by a million pounds.

> Who is able to count this idle gang who, without working, have got into their hands more than one third of your realm? The best lordships, manors and lands are theirs. Besides this they have the tenth part of all the corn, meadow, pasture, grass, wool, calves, lambs, pigs, geese and chickens. Yes, and they look so carefully at their profits that poor wives must give them every tenth egg, or else she shall be regarded as a heathen.

SOURCE 12
Extract from a book by Simon Fish criticising the Church, published in 1528.

SOURCE 13
Inside the Abbot's House at Muchelney Abbey. This was a rich monastery, worth £447 a year. The monks had been criticised for living too well, riding about the country and neglecting the church.

SOURCE 14
Front page of the *Valor Ecclesiasticus*.

THE NEW MONARCHY

ACTIVITY

Divide the class into six equal groups:

Group 1: Monks from the abbey at Bury St Edmunds (see Source 16).
Group 2: Nuns from the nunnery at Bury St Edmunds (see Source 17).
Group 3: Monks from Richard Beerely's monastery (see Source 18).
Group 4: Monks from Muchelney Abbey (see Source 13).
Group 5: Thomas Cromwell's 'Visitors'. They were chosen by him and knew that he was looking for reasons to close down monasteries and nunneries.
Group 6: People from near the religious houses in Groups 1 to 4. The visitors did not visit everywhere personally, but could take evidence from people living within ten miles. Some local people were in favour of monasteries and nunneries, some were against them.

SOURCE 15
A print showing a nun and monk.

One visitor (Group 5) and one person from Group 6 visits each of Groups 1 to 4. The monks and nuns in these groups must think what to say. Do you want your house to stay open? How are you going to defend yourself? During the visit the visitor keeps notes of what is said. At the end the visitor announces whether the monastery or nunnery is to be closed down.

'We found out nothing bad about the abbot but he often slept in monastic property away from Bury. He loved building beautiful buildings for himself. He increases the rents and shortens the LEASES of poor people who rent land from the monastery. He also keeps on with Roman Catholic CEREMONIES.'

SOURCE 16
Extract from the report of John ap Rice, Visitor to the abbey at Bury St Edmunds, to Thomas Cromwell, November 1535.

'I could not find out anything bad about the nunnery no matter how hard I tried. I believe that everybody had got together and agreed to keep things secret. Eight of the nuns will leave because they are under age. Five others would like to depart if possible.'

SOURCE 17
Extract from the report of John ap Rice, Visitor to the nunnery at Bury St Edmunds, to Thomas Cromwell, November 1535.

> My lowly and meek scribbling to your noble Grace at this time comes from my worry that the religion which we keep is no rule of St Benedict . . . The monks here have taken little notice of King Henry's command that any mention of the Pope should be crossed out of all our books. The monks drink and play bowls after breakfast until 10 o'clock or midday. They come to morning service drunk. They do nothing for the love of God. They have many other faults which I have no time to tell you about.

SOURCE 18
Extract from a letter written in 1535 to Thomas Cromwell by Richard Beerely, a monk.

Increasing royal power

With Henry as Supreme Head, the separate power of the Church was now ended. But royal control was still weak in certain parts of England and Wales.

The North

In 1536 there was a protest against the Dissolution of the Monasteries in the North, led by Robert Aske and called the Pilgrimage of Grace (see Source 19). It was crushed, but Thomas Cromwell set about increasing royal control over the North, both to prevent further rebellions and to weaken the powerful northern barons. The Council of the North, meeting in York, already existed, but was strengthened and filled with Henry's officials.

SOURCE 19
Banner carried by rebels in the 'Pilgrimage of Grace', 1536.

Wales

Edward I had conquered Wales in 1282, defeating the last independent Welsh prince and seizing his lands. Henry VII was the son of a Welshman, Edmund Tudor, and had become king in 1485 with Welsh support. Nevertheless, large parts of Wales were still ruled by marcher lords, who claimed to be independent of royal laws. Lawlessness was common.

Thomas Cromwell first appointed Rowland Lee, Bishop of Lichfield, to sort this problem out. Lee hated the Welsh and had 5,000 of them hanged. He also insisted on the Welsh using surnames, like the English did. Many Welsh names thus became Anglicised. For example, Ap Rhys (son of Rhys) became Price, Coch (Red) became Gooch or Gough and many children of Sion became Jones.

Then Cromwell made Parliament pass a series of Acts of Union between 1536 and 1543. These Acts set up a local system of law and order with separate counties (see Source 20) and Justices of the Peace, exactly as in England. Each Welsh county sent one Member of Parliament (MP) to Parliament. English law and the English language were to be used. The Acts brought law and order, as well as other benefits, but only if the Welsh abandoned some of their Welshness.

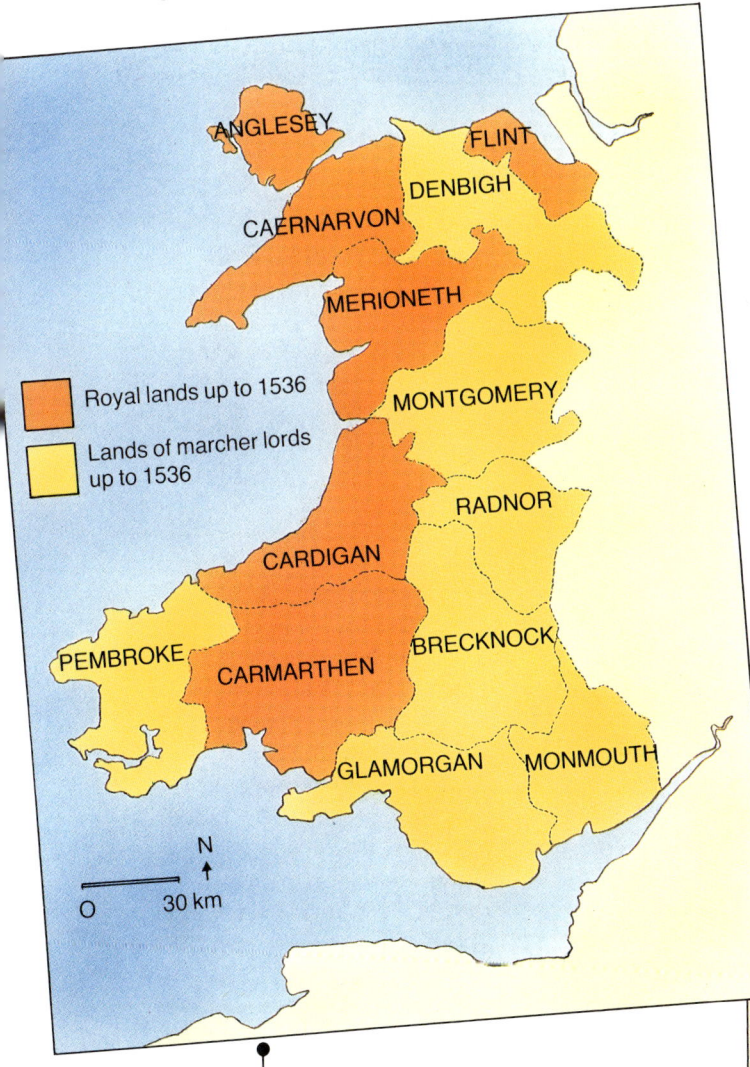

SOURCE 20
Map showing the counties of Wales created by the Act of Union 1536. These counties lasted until 1974.

Discuss this question in pairs.

What did the following gain or lose by the Acts of Union of 1536 to 1543?
a The Welsh people.
b The English government.

THE NEW MONARCHY

The Reformation in England and Wales

By the 1530s Europe was torn by arguments and wars over religion. Those who wanted change protested at the Roman Catholic Church and so were called Protestants. They wanted to reform [change] their churches, so these changes are called the Reformation.

'**1547** Jake Ball and Richard Boonde bought the silver and gold plate (used in the Roman Catholic Service). We received £15–6s (£15.30).
1548 We have whitewashed the walls of our chancel. We paid 3/- (15p).
1549 Robert Halle has made a trestle table for us and put it up in the chancel. He has removed the high stone altar. We paid 2d (1p). We have bought two new Service books in English. We paid out 7/4 (37p). Betts of Wetherden removed the organ. We paid 5/4 (27p).
1550 We bought Cranmer's New Prayer Book. We paid 20d (8p).'

SOURCE 21
Extracts from the CHURCHWARDEN's accounts from St Mary's Church, Boxford, Suffolk.

Reformation from above

Most people at that time expected their ruler to decide what their religion should be. If the ruler changed, and new ideas were brought in, most people accepted them. The early years of the Reformation in this country therefore were years of Reformation from above.

Henry VIII

Henry, like most of his people, was always a Roman Catholic at heart. He had made himself Head of the Church (see page 12) to get his divorce, but churches and church services stayed the same (see Source 22). Some of his ministers were in favour of Protestant ideas. Cromwell and Archbishop Cranmer persuaded him in 1537 to have the Bible in English placed in every church. Henry backtracked even on this, and in 1543 made it an offence to read the Bible out loud to another person.

Edward VI (1547 to 1553)

Edward was Henry's only son. Although he was only nine years old when he became king, Edward was a keen Protestant. He worked with

SOURCE 22
Inside a Roman Catholic church.

1 Rood beam
2 Cross
3 Service book in Latin
4 Priest
5 Altar
6 Candles
7 Statue of Virgin Mary
8 Stained glass windows
9 Nave (where the people worshipped)

THE NEW MONARCHY

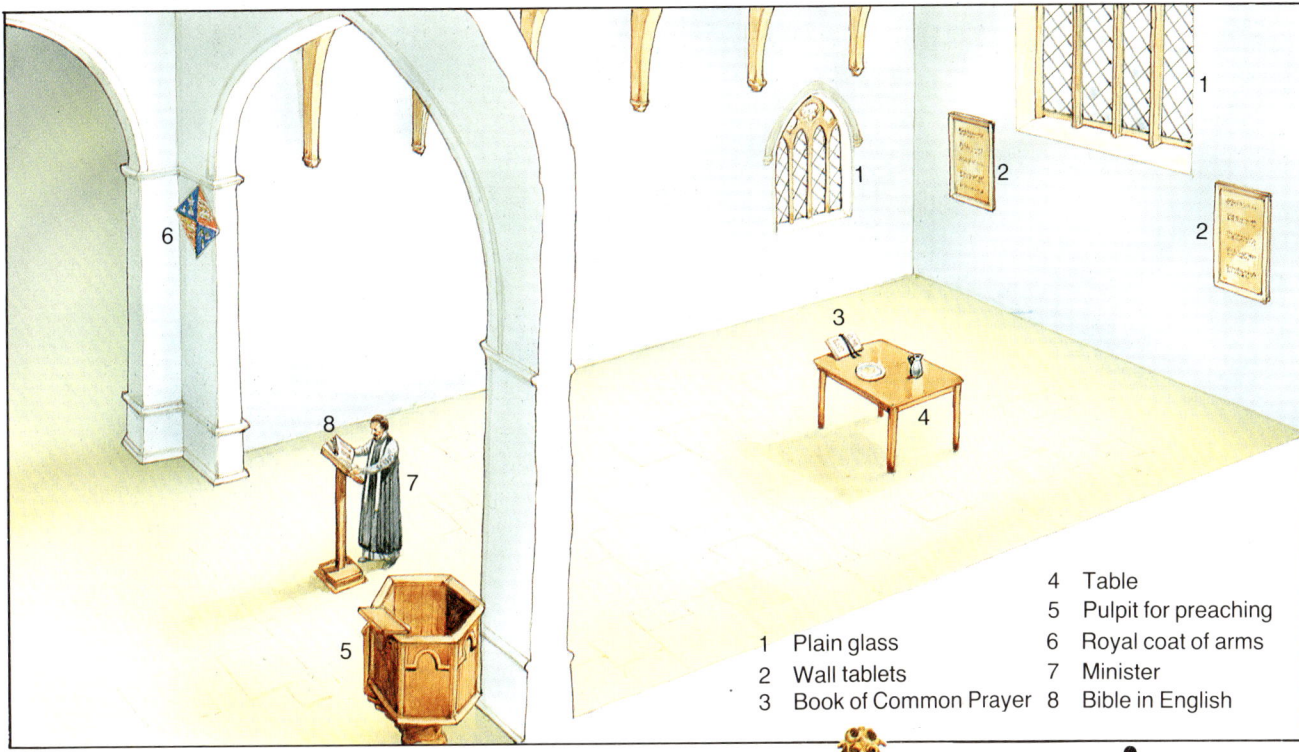

1 Plain glass
2 Wall tablets
3 Book of Common Prayer
4 Table
5 Pulpit for preaching
6 Royal coat of arms
7 Minister
8 Bible in English

SOURCE 23
Inside a Protestant church.

SOURCE 24
Medieval wood-carving of the Virgin and Child. Thousands of carvings like this were burnt by the Protestant reformers.

Archbishop Cranmer to bring in the Protestant Reformation. A new Prayer Book, in English, was issued in 1549, and another one, even more different from Roman Catholic ways, in 1552. Local people were ordered to change their churches as well (see Source 21). Protestants felt it was wrong to have pictures, statues and finely dressed priests. They wanted plain churches (see Source 23) and services in English so that they could be understood.

These changes upset many people. Many old traditions, such as local saints, Church ales, Plough Monday, holly and ivy at Christmas and tolling the church bell for the dead, were swept away. People in Devon objected so much to these changes that they rebelled (see Source 25).

SOURCE 25
Some of the demands of the rebels in the Devon Prayer Book rebellion of 1549.

'We will have statues set up again in every church and all other ceremonies used until now by our mother the holy Church . . . We will not receive the new service because it is like a Christmas game but we will have our old service in Latin as it was before, not in English.'

attainment target

1 What differences are there between the church in Source 22 and the one in Source 23?

2 What changes would you have noticed in Boxford Church if you had gone there every Sunday between 1547 and 1550?

3 How would the work of the churchwardens at Boxford be regarded by
 a Cranmer, and
 b the Devon Prayer Book rebels?

THE NEW MONARCHY

SOURCE 26
A painting of Henry VIII and his children. This is not a real scene, but is trying to give a message. Henry VIII sits in the centre with his son, Edward, kneeling before him. To the left is Mary, with her husband, King Philip of Spain, and the god of war. To the right is Elizabeth with the goddesses of peace and plenty trampling on the weapons of war.

Mary (1553 to 1558)

Mary was the daughter of Catherine of Aragon. She had been deeply affected by her mother's divorce and was determined to make England Roman Catholic again. Churches began to be changed back once more (Source 27).

There were actually very few Protestants in England at this time. In some places there was a tradition of Lollardy, which came from the 14th-century followers of John Wyclif. Protestant ideas were strongest in South-East England. This was the most properous area of the country and in closest contact with Protestants in Holland and Germany. About 800 Protestants fled abroad when Mary came to the throne.

From 1555 onwards Mary began to use the fiercest punishment of the law on Protestants who refused to become Catholics: they were burnt alive (see Source 29). Archbishop Cranmer was burnt, and four other bishops, but the statistics of the 280 people burnt show where Protestant support lay:

- 193 were burnt in London, Kent, Essex, Suffolk, Norfolk and Sussex.
- 1 in the North (Chester), 1 in the West (Exeter), 3 in Wales.
- 55 women were burnt.

'**1554** We bought a Mass book (Roman Catholic service) from London. We paid 13/8 (67p). We bought a COPE and new VESTMENTS (for the priest to wear). We paid 10/- (50p).
1555 The glazier from Hadleigh replaced some of our stained glass. 5/- (25p).
1556 To mend a cloth for the altar 2d (1p) Hartewell has put up an iron rail around the altar. We paid 5/- (25p).
1557 Childerley buys INCENSE for us. 2d (1p) New statues and paintings are put up. 20/- (£1)'.

SOURCE 27
Extracts from the churchwarden's accounts of St Mary's, Boxford, Suffolk.

THE NEW MONARCHY

Elizabeth (1558 to 1603)

Elizabeth was Anne Boleyn's daughter, connected since her birth with the break from the Pope. She could see how useful it was to be Head of the Church, and had moderate Protestant ideas. In 1559 she turned the country back to being Protestant again, more or less as it had been in the middle of Edward's reign (Source 28).

Religion and the people

So where did all these changes leave the people of England and Wales? We have seen that in Henry VIII's time most people were Roman Catholics. By the middle of Elizabeth's reign their sons and daughters were mostly Protestants. The new religion appealed to the new generation who were not so attached to the old ways. Keen Protestant preachers worked hard to persuade them. Many people were horrified at the burnings of Mary's reign. Foxe's *Book of Martyrs* was published in 1563 and even those who could not read it could understand the lurid pictures (see Source 29). William Morgan's Bible in Welsh, published in 1588, helped Protestants to spread their ideas in Wales. Devon, base of the anti-Protestant rebellion of 1549, became the breeding-ground of Protestant sailors like Francis Drake.

Puritans and Catholics

But the religious unity of the country was broken. There were some extreme Protestants, called Puritans, for whom Elizabeth did not go nearly far enough. They wanted to 'purify' the Church of any part of Roman Catholicism which still remained. They were opposed to bishops and chose their own ministers. Puritans took more part in church services, especially singing hymns.

There were also Roman Catholics. Elizabeth was a tolerant person, and her own organist, William Byrd, was a Catholic. Some Catholics went to church because they had to. John Trevelyan, a Cornish Catholic landowner, would always leave before the sermon, calling out to the priest 'When you have finished what you have to say, come and have dinner with me.'

Roman Catholic priests such as Edmund Campion were sent to England. For most of Elizabeth's reign Roman Catholicism's main supporter was Spain, England's arch-enemy. With England at war with Catholic Spain, the government thought that these priests were spies. Campion was arrested, tortured and executed.

> '1559 We have bought the new Prayer Book. We paid 5/- (25p). Roland has pulled down the altar. We paid 10d (4p). To pay for pulling down the rood loft 6/8 (33p) Lynche has made us a communion table 2/- (10p). To remove stained glass and replace it with plain glass 10/- (50p).'

SOURCE 28
Extract from the churchwarden's accounts of St Mary's, Boxford, Suffolk.

SOURCE 29
An illustration from Foxe's *Book of Martyrs* showing the burning of Thomas Hawkes, at Coggeshall, Essex, in 1555.

attainment target

1. Use Sources 27 and 28 to explain what was changed, and what remained the same in Boxford Church in the years 1554 to 1559.

2. Do you think that by 1559, after all the changes, Boxford church looked like a Catholic church or a Protestant church?

3. The 25 years from the time when Henry VIII became Head of the Church marked great changes in religion in England. In which five-year period did religion change a lot and in which five years did religion hardly change at all? Explain your answer.

4. What do you think were the most important changes in these 25 years from the point of view of: the monarch; the people of Boxford; Roman Catholics?

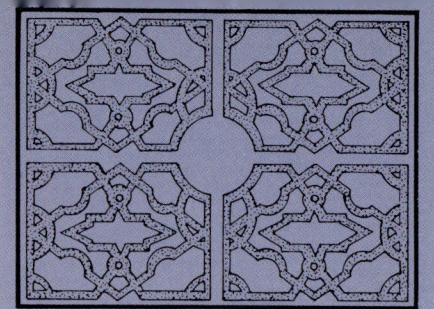

UNIT 2
People and homes

Changing styles

Montacute House, Somerset (Source 1), begun in the 1590s, was built in the latest style. If you compare it with Cothay Manor (Source 2), built in 1480, you can see just how much styles had changed.

The rooms inside were different too. Cothay Manor has a great hall where all the family and servants met and ate together; Montacute has more private rooms. Montacute has a 'parlour', a room for sitting and talking with friends, from the French *parler* (to speak). It also has gardens, perhaps with some of the new flowers brought into England in the 17th century: tulips, from Turkey; sunflowers, from Peru; and nasturtiums, from America. If the weather was wet, family and guests could exercise in the Long Gallery (Source 3).

SOURCE 1
Montacute House, Somerset.

AIMS

In this unit we will find out more about the people of England and Wales, and how they lived. We will discover who was doing well, like the owners of the houses on these pages, and who was not. We will also see how difficult it is to find accurate information about the people at this time.

PEOPLE AND HOMES

SOURCE 2
Cothay Manor, Somerset.

SOURCE 3
The Long Gallery at Montacute House.

The great rebuilding

Montacute House was built by Edward Phelips. The Dissolution of the Monasteries had meant lots of buying and selling of land. Phelips was a lawyer and had become rich by arranging these deals. He built Montacute to display his wealth.

All over England, in the years 1540 to 1640, some people were doing well and building themselves new houses. One historian has called this period 'the great rebuilding'. Successful farmers built themselves new farmhouses. Local gentry families in particular did well, often from the profits of former monastic land.

Compare Montacute House (Source 1) with Cothay Manor (Source 2). What are the differences? You could think about: size, height, size of windows, and symmetry.

SOURCE 4
Painting showing Queen Elizabeth I being carried to a wedding in June 1600.

'We in England divide our people into four groups: First there are the gentlemen. After the monarch, the first gentlemen are the lords and noblemen. After them are squires, simply called gentlemen. Second come citizens, freemen who live in the cities. Third come the yeomen. They are those who own a certain amount of land. The fourth and last group are day labourers, farmworkers, shopkeepers who have no land, and all craftsmen, such as tailors, shoemakers, carpenters, bricklayers, etc.'

SOURCE 5
Adapted from a book written by William Harrison and published in 1586.

Who were the people of England and Wales at this time? One writer, William Harrison, divided them into four groups (Source 5). Today we want better information than just a description: we want statistics. In the 16th and 17th centuries there were no government officials to collect statistics. No one thought it necessary. In the late 17th century Gregory King made rough estimates of the number of people in each group. Source 6 is a summary of his figures.

Distinctions between these groups were very strict. In the 1630s a man who said he was a better man than the Earl of Danby was put in prison and fined £2,000. There were also laws about the clothes you could wear. No one under the rank of baron could wear silver, satin or red velvet, and if a labourer wore cloth that cost more than 10d (4p) a yard, he could be put in the STOCKS for three days.

	Size of household	Total numbers	Income per year
• Gentlemen: lords, noblemen	16–40	20,000	£5,000–£800
Gentlemen: squires	8–15	134,000	£800–£300
• Citizens	5–8	250,000	£300–£100
• Yeomen	5–7	1,660,000	£100–£40
• Labourers, etc.	2–4	3,250,000	£40–£7
Vagrants, beggars, etc.	–	30,000	–

SOURCE 6
Summary of Gregory King's estimates of the people of England, published in 1696.

PEOPLE AND HOMES

Gentlemen

Nobles, lords and the richest gentlemen spent much of their time at court, with the monarch. In Source 4, Elizabeth is not being carried by servants, but by noblemen. Attendance at court was extremely expensive. You were expected to make a great show, and employ lots of servants.

When the Queen travelled about, she, and all her followers, stayed at a lord's house. This could be a great honour. If she did come, the royal party would consume as much food in a day as was normally eaten in a month.

Gentlemen like Sir Henry Tichborne (Source 8) rarely, if ever, went to court. They stayed at home and played a large part in running their county. Many became Justices of the Peace (JPs) who not only tried criminals, but fixed wages and prices. As Source 8 shows, they were like local kings. In Wales, too, farming was doing well, and the new JPs (see page 15) lived like English gentlemen.

> Parts of Wales were 'rough all over and unpleasant to see, with craggy stones, hanging rocks and ragged ways'. Elsewhere the fields were well looked after 'in some places barley, in others wheat, but generally throughout rye and afterwards four or five crops together of oats'.

SOURCE 7
Extract from *Britannia*, written by William Camden in 1586.

1 Describe the clothes worn by the people in Source 4.

2 Do you think a nobleman would think it an honour, or a disgrace, to carry the queen in this way?

3 Why do you think the queen had this painting (Source 4) made? What did she want people to think about her? What did she want people to think about the nobles?

4 Why do you think Sir Henry Tichborne had Source 8 painted?

SOURCE 8
Sir Henry Tichborne handing out bread to his household, tenants and labourers, outside his house in Hampshire.

23

PEOPLE AND HOMES

Merchants

The second group in Harrison's list (Source 5) were citizens. By 1600 perhaps one-fifth of the population of England lived in towns. London was by far the biggest, with probably 200,000 people. Norwich was next with 17,000, then York and Bristol with about 10,000 each.

In the Middle Ages the South-East of England had been much richer than the North and West. Now those areas were catching up. Totnes, Plymouth and Exeter were growing because of the cloth trade. Poole was an important port, and Newcastle was sending coal to London. Birmingham was starting to grow 'echoing with the noise of ANVILS', as William Camden put it. Leeds, Halifax and Manchester were prospering and Sheffield was becoming famous for cutlery.

Trade was still far less important than agriculture, but it was growing steadily. As more people travelled on business they needed better places to stay, to leave their horses and talk to customers. Many fine inns were built at this time, like the Feathers at Ludlow (Source 9).

Rich merchants contributed to the great rebuilding of England by building large town houses (Source 11). One such rich merchant was William Marritt of Lincoln, who died in 1616. When he died a careful list, called an inventory, was made of everything in his house. It gives us an interesting look at how he lived and furnished his house.

Source 13 shows the actual text of the inventory for one of the rooms. Source 12 gives more of the inventory and Source 10 is a plan to help you find your way round Marritt's house.

SOURCE 9
A 16th-century inn, The Feathers, at Ludlow, Shropshire.

attainment target

Read Source 12 carefully.

1. What was each of the six rooms described mainly used for?

2. How useful is Source 12 for telling us about
   a What goods he traded in?
   b How well-off he was?
   c What he was like?
   d Anything else about 17th-century England?

3. Look back at Source 6. What would you want to know about Gregory King in order to assess how reliable this source is?

4. King's figures may be wrong. Do you think we should ignore Source 6 entirely? Explain your answer.

5. Copy out this table and comment on how useful the four sources are for finding out about the people of England at this time:

	Advantages	Disadvantages
Source 5		
Source 6		
Source 8		
Source 12		

PEOPLE AND HOMES

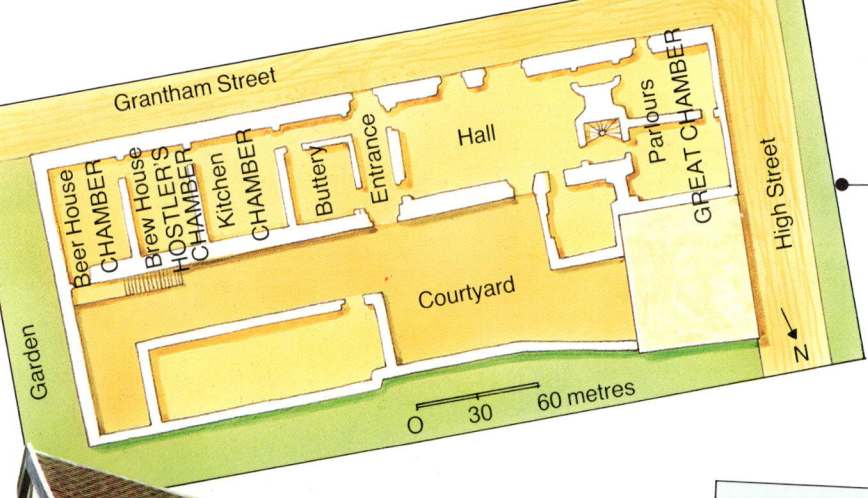

SOURCE 10
Plan of William Marritt's house. The upstairs rooms are labelled in capital letters.

SOURCE 11
William Marritt's house today.

In the parlour next the street wherein he lodged. Firstly his purse, his gown, two cloaks and his other clothes – £12. Also one bedstead, one featherbed, *bolster* and other bedding and curtains for that bed – £4. Two joined chests, one trunk, one desk and other implements 23s 4d (£1.17p). Total £17.17.

In the buttery
One hundred and two pounds of *pewter*, of pan metal thirty eight pounds, of brass candlesticks twenty pounds, six dishes, one bed pan, one *press*, two old *hutches*.

In the kitchen
Two dressers, three dripping pans, five spits, hooks.

In the brewhouse
Brewing tubs, barrels and other implements.

In the great chamber
One long table and three trestles, two bedsteads, two featherbeds, two green rugs, two pairs of curtains, two truckle bedsteads, two featherbeds, three pairs of blankets, two coverings. One square table, two chairs, one chest, six leather cushions, one other chest, one *close-stool*, twenty four pairs of sheets, six dozen napkins, twenty three pillowcases, eight table cloths, thirteen towels.

In the chamber over the kitchen
Three servant bedsteads, bedding, chairs and other furniture.

Bolster: a large pillow.
Pewter: a metal made of tin and lead, used for cups, plates, etc.
Press: for making cheese
Hutch: cupboards
Close-stool: toilet, like a commode.
The chambers were upstairs rooms.

SOURCE 12
Modern transcript of some of the inventory. (The value of items is given for the first room only.)

SOURCE 13
Part of a page of the inventory of William Marritt.

PEOPLE AND HOMES

SOURCE 14
Farm in the Lake District, dated 1629.

Yeomen

Yeomen were farmers who owned their own small farm or paid a fixed, low rent for their holding. The population of England and Wales was rising, so food prices were high and farmers did well. Their increased wealth can be seen in the many new farmhouses built between 1540 and 1640. The Lake District farmhouse in Source 14 may not look very grand, but it is solid, with glass in the windows and stone chimneys. The demand for food helped Welsh cattle farmers too. They drove their animals hundreds of miles from the Welsh hills to English markets. Welsh cattle drovers became rich and set up some of the first banks in Wales.

Yeomen farmers improved their standard of living in various other ways, as Source 16 suggests. Source 15 may be an exaggeration, but even if he was better off than a gentleman, a yeoman of Kent would always regard the gentleman as his superior.

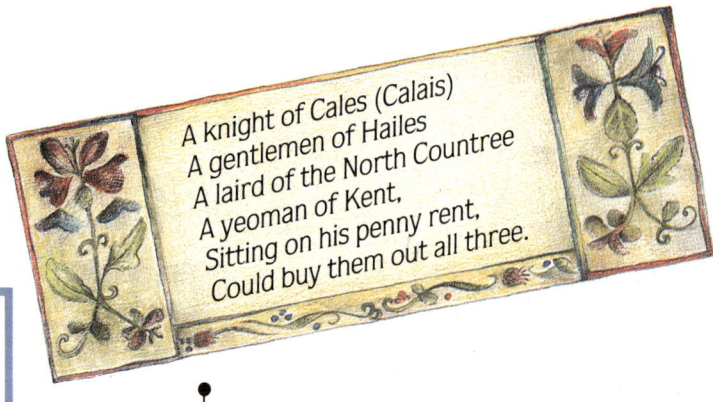

> There are old men still dwelling in the village where I live who have noted three things to be marvellously altered in England in their memory; the multitude of chimneys lately erected; the great improvement of beds . . . for we used to lie on straw sacks with a good round log for a pillow . . . and the change of vessels of wood into pewter.

SOURCE 15
A 16th-century rhyme.

A knight of Cales (Calais)
A gentlemen of Hailes
A laird of the North Countree
A yeoman of Kent,
Sitting on his penny rent,
Could buy them out all three.

SOURCE 16
An extract from a book by William Harrison, published in 1586.

PEOPLE AND HOMES

Labourers

On the whole labourers (the largest group in Source 5) were not doing very well at this time. Wages in towns were low: 1d a day for apprentice weavers, 2d a day for blacksmiths, 4d a day for master carpenters, although they often received food as well. In those days beef cost 2d a pound and a pair of shoes up to 1/- (5p).

Farmworkers toiled for long hours in the fields: 11½ hours was normal at harvest time. Their wages went up only slowly, while food prices rose quickly. Sources 18 and 19 may give rather too rosy an impression of a labourer's lifestyle.

SOURCE 17
Pewter candlestick.

SOURCE 18
Inside a labourer's cottage.

SOURCE 19
Inventory of Thomas Hearne. He was quite comfortably off although only a farmworker.

In the Hall
A table, a bench, a plank, two chairs, two shelves and painted cloths.
Brass: one pot, three kettles, two pans, a basin, two candlesticks.
Pewter: four plates, two bowls, a salt cellar, a saucer.
A bowl, a pair of bellows, dishes.

Chamber
An old bedstead, a cupboard, an old chest and painted cloths. Apples worth 10/- (50p). An axe, a hatchet, a wedge, a *billhook*, a spit, a pair of *andirons* and pot-hangers.

Chamber in the entry (on the landing?)
A plain bedstead, a flocked bolster and a coverlet. An old bedstead, a chest and a tub.

Kitchen
A tub, three boards, two spinning wheels, a grindstone and pot-hangers.

Barn
Wheat and barley worth £4.15 (£4.75p). Hay and feed worth £1.
Ladders, sieves and other lumber. One cow and two young bullocks worth £2.10.
Crops in the ground this year worth £1.10 (£1.50p).

Billhook: a curved knife on a pole.
Andirons: for holding logs in a fireplace.

ACTIVITY

Look at Source 19. Working in pairs, make sure you understand what everything in the inventory is, what it looked like and how it was used. Use a dictionary and the library to help you.

1. Try to draw a room in Thomas Hearne's house, or imagine Thomas or his wife showing you around their cottage. Remember that every single thing of value they had is in the inventory.

2. What can you tell from this inventory about the life of Thomas Hearne and his wife? What would it be like to live there? Remember that although they are among the better-off farmworkers in the village, many yeomen and gentlemen were far richer. Remember also that Thomas and his wife accepted this as the way things were.

3. Act out, or write, some episodes in a day in the life of Thomas Hearne and his wife.

PEOPLE AND HOMES

SOURCE 20
Hardwick Hall.

'The paradise of married women'

It was not just men who built houses to show off their wealth. Source 20 shows the front of Hardwick Hall in Derbyshire, one of the most spectacular Elizabethan houses in England, begun in 1591. The letters E S round the roof stand for Elizabeth, Countess of Shrewsbury (Source 21), who had it built. She had become very rich as a result of four marriages to wealthy men, who left their money to her when they died.

'Bess of Hardwick' as she was called, was hardly typical. What was life really like for women in the period 1540 to 1640? A Dutchman who knew England well described the lives of women that he saw, and called England 'A paradise of married

SOURCE 21
Elizabeth, Countess of Shrewsbury, 'Bess of Hardwick'.

PEOPLE AND HOMES

women' (see Source 22). The other sources on these pages will help you decide if he was right.

As with men, the lives of women depended very much on how rich they were. Poorer women were expected to work hard at their own tasks and help their husbands too – see Source 23 and also Source 18 (page 27).

Working women obviously made important contributions to the survival of the family, both working alongside their husbands and on their own.

One task which always fell to women was caring for people in times of crisis, such as childbirth, death or illness. Only rich people used doctors. Women in the village passed round recipes for medicines and cures. They had practical skills, especially in midwifery (Source 25) which were essential.

> Wives in England are entirely in the power of their husbands, yet they are not kept so strictly as in Spain. Nor are they shut up . . . They go to market to buy what they like best to eat. They are well-dressed, fond of taking it easy and leave the care of the household to their STEWARDS. They sit in front of their doors, dressed in fine clothes, to see and be seen by passers-by. In all banquets and feasts they are shown the highest honour . . . All the rest of the time they spend in walking and riding, in playing at cards, in visiting their friends, conversing with their neighbours and making merry with them and childbirths and christenings. And all this with the permission of their husbands. This is why England is called the paradise of married women.

SOURCE 22
Extract from a book published in 1575 and written by a Dutch merchant, Van Meteren, living in London.

SOURCE 23
Extract from a book about farming, written by Anthony FitzHerbert in 1523.

'It is a wife's occupation to winnow corn, make malt, make hay, and in time of need to help her husband to fill the muck wagon, drive the plough, load hay or corn . . . to go to market to sell butter, cheese, milk, eggs, hens, geese.'

'Took horse and rode to Harwoodall to see our farm be bought . . . I walked with Mr Hoby about the town to spy out the best places where cottages might be built . . . After supper I talked a good deal with Mr Hoby of farming and household matters.'

SOURCE 24
Extract from the diary of Lady Hoby.

SOURCE 25
Midwife attending at childbirth.

attainment target

1 Do you agree that the life described in Source 22 is 'a paradise for married women'?

2 What are the advantages and disadvantages of using a description written by a foreign observer? Do you think we are dealing here with facts or opinions?

3 How much do the following sources support or contradict Van Meteren's views: Source 18, 20, 23, 24 and 25.

4 Which of these sources might Van Meteren have chosen to support his view?

5 Do you think England at this time was 'the paradise of married women'?

PEOPLE AND HOMES

SOURCE 26
Begging in London today.

SOURCE 27
A beggar and a gentleman: an illustration of 1569.

Beggars and vagabonds

What do members of your class feel about people begging, as in Source 26? Our reactions are usually divided between those who think beggars should be made to find work, and those who think they should be helped by the government. The same problems, and the same suggestions for answers, could be found in England 400 years ago.

At that time the number of people who were poor and out of work seemed to be increasing. Some turned to begging, some to crime. There was no unemployment benefit, but people who were disabled and so could not work were allowed to beg. Those who could work and didn't were called vagabonds, and punished. In 1572 the law was toughened up: vagabonds were to be whipped and burned through the gristle of the right ear. This was frequently carried out (see Source 28). The government did this for two reasons:

- They believed that not working was wicked and sinful.
- They were worried about law and order. There was no police force and gangs of vagabonds could do as they pleased.

'29 March 1573. At Harrow Hill in Middlesex, John Allan, Elizabeth Turner, Humphrey Foxe, Henry Bower and Agnes Vat, being over 14 years of age and having no lawful means of livelihood, were declared vagabonds. Sentenced to be FLOGGED and burnt through the right ear.'

SOURCE 28
An item from the records of Middlesex, dated 1573.

The rise in unemployment

People at the time blamed many things for the rising numbers of unemployed people: gambling, overspending by the rich, wars with Spain or the Dissolution of the Monasteries which used to look after beggars and vagabonds. Most of all they blamed ENCLOSURES. The growth of the cloth trade meant that sheep farming was profitable. Some landowners stopped arable farming (Source 29) and turned their farms into sheep-walks (Source 30). A comparison of the two pictures shows what effect this had on the number of people employed.

PEOPLE AND HOMES

We have already seen that there were no accurate statistics. Modern historians have pointed out that enclosure for sheep farming actually declined in the late 16th century. They also say that the population was rising fast, so there simply was not enough work for everyone.

The Elizabethan Poor Law

By the end of the 16th century it was clear that harsh laws were not stopping vagabonds. The situation was worst in towns. Some of them, such as Ipswich (Source 31), had a different attitude. Eventually the government passed the great Poor Law of 1601, which lasted until 1834. This said:

- Poor people had to stay in their own parish and not wander about.
- Each parish must look after its own poor, and could collect a local tax, the poor rate, to do this.
- Disabled poor would be looked after in their own houses, out of the poor rate.
- Able-bodied poor would be looked after, but would be given work to do.
- Poor children would also be looked after and taught a trade.

The 1601 Poor Law was quite a change. It seemed to acccept that it was not the people's fault if they were poor. It raised money from more fortunate people to look after the poor, in different ways.

SOURCE 29
A 16th-century illustration of harvesting.

SOURCE 30
A 16th-century illustration of a sheep-walk.

'Wednesday, 2 December 1551. Two in every parish shall be nominated by the bailiffs to enquire into the poor of the parish.

Monday, 22 February 1557. No children of this town shall be permitted to beg. Those adults that shall be permitted to beg shall have badges.

Monday, 26 September 1569. The late house of Blackfriars, bought of John Southwell, shall be henceforth a hospital for the poor people of this town and shall be called Christ's Hospital.'

SOURCE 31
Extracts from Ipswich town records.

Discuss your answers to these questions in groups of four.

1. Look at Source 26. What are your views on begging? Do you give money to beggars? Should the government help these people?

2. What are the similarities and differences between the situations in Sources 26 and 27?

3. What were the attitudes of the government to the problems of the poor
   a in 1572?
   b in 1601?

4. How do these attitudes compare with those of the government today?

UNIT 3

Kings and Parliaments

Uniting the crowns, 1603

King James VI of Scotland became King James I of England in 1603. He was the son of Mary Queen of Scots and the great grandson of Henry VIII's sister, Margaret. Born in 1566, he had become King of Scotland in the next year. He was therefore already an experienced monarch when he took the English throne. As he travelled south to London he was welcomed by the English. Yet only 39 years later the people of Britain were divided by a terrible civil war. At the end of this civil war, James's son Charles was executed for having caused it. What went wrong? How did the joy and unity of 1603 turn into the bitterness and bloodshed of 1642?

AIMS

A CIVIL WAR is a war between different groups inside a country. In this unit you will discover what went wrong in England to cause the outbreak of the Civil War in 1642. You will know by now that complex events usually have several causes. Some historians think that the long-term causes of the Civil War go back at least to 1603, perhaps earlier. You will find out about these long-term causes, as well as the short-term causes in the years up to 1642. The unit ends by looking at who won the Civil War and why.

SOURCE 1
James in 1595, aged 29.

SOURCE 2
The execution of Charles I in 1649, from a print made at the time.

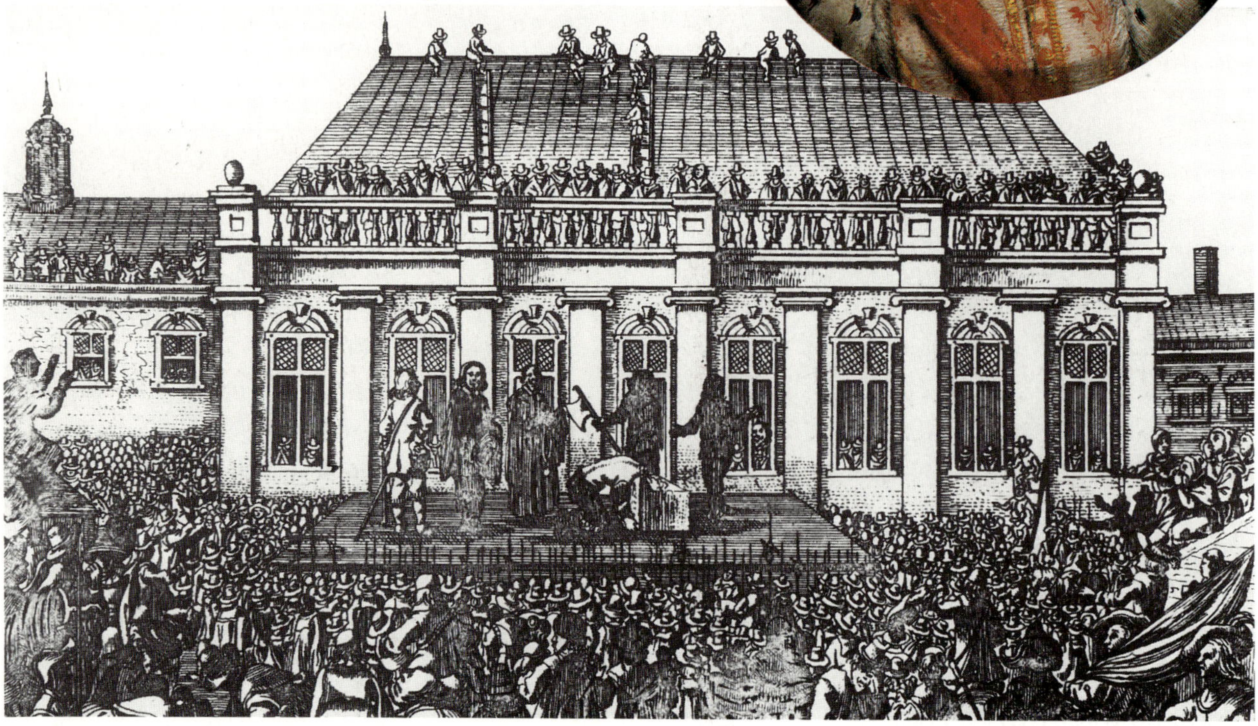

KINGS AND PARLIAMENTS

SOURCE 3
The Gunpowder Plotters.

Two kingdoms, one king

James was King of England and Scotland. The two countries continued to be separate, as they had been for centuries, linked only by having the same king. One Englishman hated this and said it was like being tied to a dead body and thrown into a ditch. James wanted to unite the two kingdoms but Parliament refused. Nevertheless, as we shall see, England and Scotland did draw closer together over the 17th century.

The Gunpowder Plot 1605

To Roman Catholics, James, a Protestant, was not the rightful king. A group of them plotted to kill him, and many lords and MPs, by blowing up the Houses of Parliament. James's ministers may have known about the plot and used it to stir up anti-Catholic feeling. They waited until they could catch all the plotters, then, on 5 November 1605, Guy Fawkes was arrested and the plot revealed.

Coming after the burning of Protestants in Mary's reign, and the attempted invasion of England by the Spanish Armada in 1588, the Gunpowder Plot increased hatred and fear of Roman Catholics. After 1688 (see unit 4) 5 November was celebrated as Guy Fawkes night. In some places (see Source 4) this has remained an anti-Catholic celebration right up to this century.

SOURCE 4
Guy Fawkes Night in Lewes, Sussex.

1 In 1603 James had already been a successful king of Scotland for 36 years. Do you think this was an advantage or a disadvantage to him in becoming King of England?

2 Why do you think the Gunpowder Plot helped James become more popular?

KINGS AND PARLIAMENTS

The Divine Right of Kings

The Scottish lords had not been easy to rule, so James emphasised royal power. He said that monarchs were chosen by God to govern and could do what they liked or needed to do. This idea was called the DIVINE RIGHT of Kings (see Source 5). James and his son, Charles, used the best ARCHITECTS and artists of their time to support this view of royal power, as Sources 6 and 7 show.

As we saw in unit 1, in Henry VIII's time most people accepted the idea of an all-powerful monarch. The trouble was that England had changed since then. Misunderstandings and disagreements grew up between James and his people. The main issues were *religion*, *Parliament* and *money*.

> It is not lawful to argue with the King's power. It is contempt in a subject to say that a King cannot do this or that. Kings are the makers of laws . . . and as the King is overlord of the whole land so he has power of life and death over every person that lives in the same.

SOURCE 5
James's idea of monarchy, from a book he wrote in 1603.

Discuss these questions in pairs.

1. How do you react to James's views on the Divine Right of Kings in Source 5?
2. Give three words which describe the interior of the Banqueting House (Sources 6 and 7).
3. How does the design of the Banqueting House build up the power and dignity of the king?

SOURCE 6
Inside the Banqueting House in Whitehall, designed by Inigo Jones in 1619. James met important visitors here, sitting in state.

SOURCE 7
Huge ceiling painting by Rubens in the Banqueting House. It shows James being lifted up to Heaven.

Religion

The Puritans wanted to make England more Protestant than Elizabeth had allowed (see unit 1). They believed that every person had his or her own relationship with God so there was no need for bishops or priests. Scotland was a very Puritan country, so they had high hopes that James would change things. In fact James hated the Puritans of Scotland because they had tried to tell him what to do. He supported bishops and told the Puritans they must accept this or he would 'harry them out of the land'. Some Puritans did leave, such as the Pilgrim Fathers who went to North America in 1620, but many stayed and resented James's attitude.

Parliament

Unlike Scotland where the barons were still important, the most important people in England were the country gentlemen. They ran affairs in their counties and met in the House of Commons. The Scottish Parliament was weak, but the English Parliament, especially the House of Commons, had gradually increased its power. Members of Parliament had been consulted about all the great religious changes of the 16th century. They met more often. The taxes they could grant to the monarch became more and more necessary (see next page). In some of her Parliaments MPs had disagreed with Elizabeth. However, Elizabeth had generally taken note of their views and was trusted by them as a result.

James made little effort to consult them or win their trust. He could hardly believe they would dare to criticise him (see Source 8). He pointed out, quite correctly, that monarchs had the right to call and dismiss Parliaments as they pleased. His response to criticism was to lecture them about Divine Right, on which he considered himself an expert.

James preferred to work with his personal favourites. The most powerful of these was the Duke of Buckingham, or 'Steenie' as James called him. From 1618 to 1628 Steenie really ruled England alongside James and Charles. Some of the many honours and titles he was given are listed next to his portrait (Source 9).

'At their meetings nothing is heard but cries, shouts and confusion. I am surprised that my ANCESTORS should have allowed such an institution to come into existence.'

SOURCE 8
James's views on the House of Commons.

SOURCE 9
George Villiers, Duke, Marquis and Earl of Buckingham, Earl of Coventry, Viscount Villiers, Baron of Whadden, Great Admiral of the kingdom of England and Ireland.

KINGS AND PARLIAMENTS

Money

England was a richer country than Scotland, so James thought that he would be better off when he became king. In fact royal income had risen in value only three times since the 1530s, from £200,000 to £600,000 a year, while prices had risen five or six times. The money from the Dissolution of the Monasteries had been spent on wars and the monastic lands sold off to raise money. Parliament could have granted James more money from taxes, but was reluctant to do so.

James spent money on himself, his family, his friends and on grand entertainment, at a great rate. His household cost £35,000 a year to run, while Elizabeth's had cost only £9,500. Buckingham's foreign wars proved expensive. To make ends meet, James found other sources of income. He had the right to grant titles, so he invented a new one – baronet – and sold it at £1,000 each.

He also had the right to grant monopolies, which was the exclusive right to sell certain goods. Monopolies put up prices and annoyed other traders. James sold over 100 monopolies, including bricks, coal, butter, currants, herrings, tobacco, dice, coaches, hay, belts, buttons, even mousetraps.

Charles I

Charles I (Source 10) was a quiet, mild, but obstinate man. He was a firm believer in the Divine Right of Kings, and had much the same views as his father on Parliament.

ACTIVITY

Get into groups of three or four for this activity, which is in two parts.

1 Judgement on James
Look back over this unit so far, and answer the following questions:
  a What things had James misunderstood about England and the English?
  b What things had the English misunderstood about James?
  c When James died in 1625 relations between him and some English people were tense, but it was nowhere near a civil war. Who was to blame for the tension?

Copy and fill in the table below:

Issues on which James was entirely to blame	Issues on which James was partly to blame	Issues on which James was not to blame at all

2 Advice to Charles
What advice would you give to Charles at the beginning of his reign to help him rule peacefully and successfully? You should include advice on how to handle the three key issues: religion, Parliament, money.

SOURCE 10
Charles I, a painting by Van Dyck from 1635. This painting shows Charles from three different angles.

KINGS AND PARLIAMENTS

SOURCE 11
Henrietta Maria, Charles's French, Roman Catholic wife.

'Our treasures exhausted and our COFFERS empty, we summoned a Parliament, but not finding that success therein which we had just hope to expect, we are resolved to require the aid of our good and loving subjects by lending us a sufficient sum of money to be repaid them as soon as we shall be in any way able to do so.'

SOURCE 12
Charles asking for loans, 1627 (adapted).

Read Source 12 carefully.

1. What reasons does Charles give for asking for these loans?
2. If you received one of these letters from Charles, did you have a choice over whether you lent him money?
3. When would you be paid back?
4. Would *you* have lent the king money in this situation?

After the assassination of Buckingham in 1628, Charles began to rely heavily on his wife, Henrietta Maria (Source 11). This worried many people: she was a princess from France, where kings ruled with complete power. She, and the friends she brought with her from France, were Roman Catholic.

Charles quarrelled with his first Parliament. He needed money to run the country, but Parliament refused to grant him any unless he agreed to their demands. He therefore dismissed Parliament and began to raise money by other means, such as forcing rich people to lend him some (see Source 12).

The Petition of Right

In 1628 war with France broke out and Charles had to call another Parliament. Parliamentary leaders such as John Pym (Source 13) forced him to sign a document called the Petition of Right. This said he would not collect taxes without their permission or arrest people without trial. To Pym and many MPs, Charles was using his powers in a new way, to set up one-person royal rule. To Charles, Parliament was going beyond anything it had ever done before. He dismissed it in 1629 and began to rule without it.

SOURCE 13
John Pym, Somerset MP, wealthy landowner and merchant. Like many MPs he was a Puritan, educated at university and trained as a lawyer. He first became an MP in 1614 and became a leading critic first of James, then Charles.

MAKING CONNECTIONS

Styles of monarchy

In monarchies, where the whole system revolves round one person, the character of that person is obviously important. Are they intelligent, brave, tactful, just, hard-working? Or are they stupid, cowardly, unfair, lazy and overbearing? All monarchs faced problems — shortage of money, dissatisfied courtiers or parliaments, enemies abroad, and, occasionally, rebels at home. Sometimes they handled these problems well — like Queen Elizabeth I — and won praise and popularity. Sometimes they decided on disastrous policies which eventually lost them their thrones. As you read through this book, consider how the characters of the kings of England and France influenced events during their reigns.

SOURCE 14
Charles I on horseback, painted by Van Dyck in 1633.

SOURCE 15
The Queen's House, Greenwich.

What was Charles I like?

Charles and religion
He remained a staunch Anglican all his life. In spite of what his opponents might have feared, he was never tempted to join his wife in the Roman Catholic church.

Charles and English history
In spite of what his opponents said, he did not break the law. He believed in the Divine Right of kings to rule but that did not mean he thought he could do what he liked. He believed that he should only use those powers which kings of England had always had. The problem was that he went ahead with actions that were lawful but also very unpopular.

Charles and the arts
Like many European monarchs, Charles was a great patron of the arts. He had his own orchestra, he built up a vast royal collection of sculptures and paintings and he invited some of the great European artists of his day to England to work for him, including Rubens and Van Dyck, see Source 14. He asked the famous architect Inigo Jones to design rooms and buildings for him, see Source 15.

Charles the family man
His marriage to Henrietta Maria (see Source 11 on page 37) was arranged, and although at first they did not get on, later they became very close. Charles was fond of his children: his farewell to his three younger children while he was a prisoner in 1647 moved even Cromwell to tears.

MAKING CONNECTIONS

The 'Sun King'

In France, Cardinal Richelieu (Source 16) ruled for King Louis XIII. Richelieu successfully built up the power of the crown, removing all rivals. The Estates-General, the nearest France had to a Parliament, met in 1614 and were not called again until 1789 (see page 74). Thanks to Richelieu's hard work, Louis XIV, the next king, was able to make himself the centre of all power and influence. He called himself the 'Sun King', see Source 17.

Charles and other people
He was a quiet, cold, shy man. He could be ungrateful to his friends and did not try to win over his enemies. He did not try to be popular. He believed that kings were appointed by God to rule; they were not like other men. As King Louis XIV of France (1643 to 1715) said, 'I am the nation' (l'état c'est moi).

Charles and Europe.
Charles' ideas on how to rule, like his ideas on art and architecture, were held by most rulers in Europe at the time. The kings of France and Spain, the emperors of Austria, the rulers of the little states of Italy and Germany all believed in Divine Right. He was more in step with his time than were his opponents in Parliament.

Charles' court
He put an end to the drunkenness and rowdiness of his father's court. He admired the strict ceremonial of the Spanish court he had visited in 1623 and made his own more dignified.

Charles' physique
He had been a weak child and did not grow up to be tough-looking. However he could swim, dance and play tennis. In the Civil War he rode on horseback for many hours without tiring. He fought in the battle of Edgehill and would have led his cavalry in a charge at the battle of Naseby if he had not been prevented.

SOURCE 16
Cardinal Richelieu, Chief Minister (1624 to 1642) to King Louis XIII of France.

SOURCE 17
Louis XIV, King of France, 1643 to 1715.

ACTIVITY

Look through the eight aspects of Charles' character. Reach your own judgement on him by giving points out of five on each of the eight aspects. Go through once, judging him as a person: what would it be like to meet him?

Then judge him as a monarch: look through the eight aspects and decide which are the two most important. Mark these out of 20. Now decide on the three next most important: mark these out of 10. Mark the rest out of five as before. Now award him marks out of the new totals. Write a short biography of Charles I on the basis of your marks.

KINGS AND PARLIAMENTS

Charles's personal rule 1629 to 1638

If Charles was going to rule without Parliament, he obviously had to cut his costs and raise money. War was his most expensive activity, so he made peace with France and Spain. He used various methods of raising extra money:

- CUSTOMS duties. Parliament normally granted the monarch the right to collect these for life, but the Parliament of 1625 had refused. Charles asked for their collection anyway (see Source 18).
- Forced loans (see Source 12, page 37).
- Monopolies (see page 36).
- Fines. The king had the right to collect fines from law courts. Charles looked into old laws, such as the forest laws, and fined people for breaking them.
- Ship money. Coastal counties had sometimes been taxed to provide ships for the navy. In 1634 Charles made this a regular tax and in 1635 extended it to the whole country. This seemed only fair: why shouldn't inland areas pay for the defence of the nation? Many people opposed ship money. A Buckinghamshire gentleman, John Hampden, was sent to prison for refusing to pay (Source 19).

Ship money raised £730,000 between 1634 and 1640. Charles seemed to be able to rule without ever having to call Parliament again. But although he had enough income to rule, he did not have enough for a war.

SOURCE 19
Statue of John Hampden in Aylesbury town centre.

'Finding that it hath continued for many ages and is now an important part of the revenue of the Crown, but could not be settled by Parliament by reason of the dissolution of Parliament, we have therefore ordered that all duties upon goods and MERCHANDISE should be levied in such a manner as were levied in the time of our late dear father King James.'

SOURCE 18
Letter from Charles about customs duties, 1625 (adapted).

Discuss these questions in pairs.

1 Which groups of people would be annoyed by each of Charles's methods of raising money?

2 Who do you feel was behaving unreasonably in the first 13 years of Charles's reign (1625 to 1638): Charles? Parliament? Both? Neither?

3 Do you think governments should tax people?

KINGS AND PARLIAMENTS

SOURCE 21
A cartoon printed at the time showing Laud eating the ears of William Prynne, a Puritan who had been sentenced to have his ears cut off for criticising Laud's reforms.

SOURCE 20
Church furnished in the way favoured by Charles and Laud.

William Laud

Some people, such as William Laud, believed that the Church of England was too Protestant. They wanted to bring back stained glass windows, a railed-off altar at the east end of the church, more ritual and special clothes for priests (see Source 22). Charles supported this and in 1633 made Laud Archbishop of Canterbury.

The Puritans were very angry at this, but those who protested too much were imprisoned or treated harshly (see Source 21). Then Charles and Laud made a serious mistake: they introduced their ideas into Scotland. If English Puritans were angry, the Scots were furious. The whole country united, thousands signed a National Covenant and formed an army.

Charles called a Parliament and asked for money for an army to crush the Scots. In Parliament John Pym insisted on Charles changing his rule before they would grant a penny. Charles dismissed them, but the Scots invaded England and he had to offer them £850 a day not to move any further south. His policy was in ruins, and he called Parliament again.

'This year being Laud's first as Archbishop of Canterbury, great offence was taken when he set up pictures in the windows of his palaces at Lambeth and Croydon, and at his bowing towards the altar which all the people protested against as being POPISH. Mr Ward, a minister in Ipswich preached against bowing at the mention of Jesus' name, for which he was committed to prison, where he lay a long time.'

SOURCE 22
Reactions to Laud's reforms, described by J Rushworth in 1701.

1. Compare Source 20 with the two styles of church in Unit 1: Source 22, page 16 and Source 23, page 17. Do you think the Puritans were right in thinking that Laud was bringing back Roman Catholic ways?
2. Make a list of things Puritans objected to in Laud's reforms.

KINGS AND PARLIAMENTS

The drift to civil war

No one wanted a civil war. Charles's attempt to rule on his own was over and he had to do what Parliament wanted. But he was furious with what the Parliamentary leaders were doing, and looked for ways of turning the tables on them.

The first thing Parliament did was to put Laud and the Earl of Strafford in the Tower of London. Strafford had been an MP who changed sides and helped Charles rule. He had been a tough and efficient ruler of the North, then of Ireland. Pym had him put on trial by both Houses of Parliament on a charge of treason (Source 23). The Commons voted by 204 to 59 that he was guilty, the Lords by 26 to 19, and he was executed.

Parliament then set about weakening royal power and strengthening its own. Ship money and forced loans were abolished. Parliament had to meet every three years, and could not be dissolved without its own consent.

By this time many MPs were becoming worried by what Pym was up to. They disliked the mob violence in the streets of London and the continued criticism of the king. They feared that attacks on the king could lead to attacks on the upper classes. Charles went to Scotland and began to gather support there.

Then, with Strafford out of the way, there was a massive rebellion in Ireland. Charles returned to London to ask Parliament for an army to put it down. Parliament feared what Charles might do in England if he had an army and refused. Pym drew up the Grand Remonstrance: a list of all the grievances Parliament had against Charles. It was passed, but the voting was close: 159 to 148.

SOURCE 23
The Trial of the Earl of Strafford, 1641, by both Houses of Parliament. The Lords are on the right, Commons on the left, Strafford is in the centre with his back to us.

KINGS AND PARLIAMENTS

The five members

Encouraged by this, Charles came to Parliament with soldiers to arrest Pym and four other leading MPs (see Source 24). They had heard of his plans and escaped down the river into the City of London. Charles's action seemed to prove that he could not be trusted.

Charles moved out of London and began to look for support. In August 1642 he raised his flag at Nottingham and called on all loyal subjects of military age to join him. Some, like Edward Hyde (see Source 26) were convinced he was in the right; others, like Sir Edmund Verney, were not at all convinced, but fought for him out of sheer old-fashioned loyalty to the Crown. Parliament also prepared for war. Among those who took up arms for Parliament was Sir Edmund's son, Sir Ralph Verney. The Civil War had begun.

'The King came for those five gentlemen. Then he called Mr Pym by name, and no answer was made. Then he asked the Speaker if they were there or where they were.

Upon that the Speaker fell on his knees and said that he was a servant of the House and neither had eyes nor tongue to hear or say anything but what Parliament commanded. Then the King told him he thought that his eyes were as good as his, and then said his birds had flown but he did expect the House would send them to him. He assured us they would have a fair trial, and so went out.'

SOURCE 24
Extract from a letter written by Sir Ralph Verney, describing Charles's attempt to arrest the five MPs, January 1642.

SOURCE 25
17th-century print of Charles raising his standard (flag) at Nottingham, August 1642.

'You have the satisfaction of believing you are in the right, that the King ought not to grant what is required of him. But for my part I do not like the quarrel and wish the King would consent to what they desire. My only concern now is to follow my master. I have served him for 30 years and will not do so base a thing as to desert him now.'

SOURCE 26
Sir Edmund Verney's words just before his death at the battle of Edgehill, October 1642, recorded by his friend Edward Hyde. Sir Edmund Verney was Sir Ralph's father.

attainment target

1. Give one reason why some people chose to fight for:
   a. the king and
   b. Parliament.

2. Divide your page into three columns with the headings shown. Fill in as many causes under each heading as you can.

Causes which go back before 1629	Causes which go back before 1640	Causes which emerged after 1640

3. For each cause you have chosen write the letter P, R, S or E against it, to say whether you think it was:
   Political (P) – to do with the actions of kings or Parliament
   Religious (R) – to do with the Church and styles of worship
   Economic (E) – to do with money and trade
   Social (S) – to do with different types of people in society.

4. Are any of these types of cause linked together? Explain one such link.

5. Which type of cause (political, religious, economic or social) do you think was the most important? Explain your answer.

43

KINGS AND PARLIAMENTS

The division of England

The arguments between king and Parliament split the country (Source 28). They even split families, and old friends found themselves fighting one another (see Source 29). Many people, however, had nothing to do with the fighting. The marching armies and their demands for food disrupted trade and farming. In Dorset and Somerset the 'Clubmen' took up arms against both sides to keep them out of their areas.

The king's support came from the more traditional areas and the old nobility. Many of these were skilled horsemen and used to weapons. They were called 'cavaliers', which means horsemen. The king's nephew, Prince Rupert, led the Royalist cavalry with great success in early battles.

Parliament's supporters came mainly from lesser gentry, townspeople and merchants (see Source 30). The backing of apprentice boys who had short hair gave them their nickname of 'roundheads'. But Parliament had three great advantages which would help it in the long run:
- South-East England was richer, and so could pay for a long war.
- The Navy supported Parliament, so it was difficult for the king to get men and supplies from abroad.
- Before he died in December 1642, Pym set up a well-organised system to supply Parliament's army with money.

SOURCE 28
How the country divided in the Civil War.

'The experience I have had of your worth and the happiness I have enjoyed in your friendship are wounding considerations when I look at this present distance between us. My affection for you is unchangeable, but I must be true to the cause in which I serve. The great God knows with what a sad sense I go upon this service and with what a perfect hatred I detest this war without an enemy. Your most affectionate friend, and faithful servant, William Waller.'

SOURCE 29
Extract from a letter from William Waller to Ralph Hopton, 1643 (adapted). The men were old friends. William Waller was a general on Parliament's side; Ralph Hopton was a Royalist general.

'A people of inferior degree who by good farming, the cloth trade and other thriving businesses had gotten very good fortunes, were fast friends to Parliament.'

SOURCE 30
This sentence describing Somerset is from *The History of the Great Rebellion*, by the royalist Edward Hyde, Lord Clarendon.

KINGS AND PARLIAMENTS

The New Model Army

We read in Source 26 that Sir Edmund Verney took up arms reluctantly. The same was true on Parliament's side: some people were unsure if they should defeat their king in battle. This was no way to fight a war.

Oliver Cromwell, the MP for Cambridge, began to show his skill as cavalry commander of the parliamentary army from East Anglia. He promoted people for their ability, not for how important they were (see Source 31). He allowed Puritans of all kinds to worship in whatever way they wanted. He himself believed that God was on his side, and saw proof of this in his victories (see Source 32). In return he expected loyalty, good discipline and strict training from his men.

In 1644 Parliament set up the New Model Army. This defeated the king at Marston Moor in 1644 and at Naseby in 1645 (Source 33). At Naseby it was Cromwell's disciplined cavalry, halting their charge and attacking the Royalist infantry, which turned the battle. By then the Scots had joined in on Parliament's side and the king was facing defeat. He surrendered to the Scots in 1646 and they handed him over to the English. Charles talked terms with the Army, but in 1647 he escaped and made a deal with the Scots. Cromwell defeated the Scots and Royalists at the battle of Preston in 1648.

> Give me a russet-coated captain that knows what he fights for and loves what he knows than that which you call a gentleman and is nothing else.

SOURCE 31
Oliver Cromwell describes his attitude to promotion in the New Model Army.

> I could not, riding about my business, but smile out to God in praises, in assurance of victory.

SOURCE 32
Cromwell, speaking before the battle of Naseby.

SOURCE 33
The forces before the battle of Naseby, 1645. The Royalist army is at the top, with the king in front of it. Prince Rupert's cavalry is on the Royalist right. The Parliamentary Army is at the bottom, commanded by Sir Thomas Fairfax. Oliver Cromwell is on the right.

AIMS

In this unit we will see that putting the king on trial and executing him posed all kinds of problems. Over the years 1649 to 1714 many people tried to find a government which had both the right and the power to rule. There were short periods when things seemed to be working out, but soon they went wrong again. We will learn about some of these ideas for government in this unit.

We will also find out how these dramatic events in England had important effects on Scotland and Ireland. You will see why this section is called *The Making of the United Kingdom*.

UNIT 4

Searching for a settlement

We saw at the end of unit 3 that some people on Parliament's side were not sure about fighting against their king. We also saw that Cromwell and the New Model Army had no such doubts. They thought that Charles had been untrustworthy and unreasonable. They blamed him for the war and called him 'the man of blood'. They feared that as long as he was alive another outbreak of civil war was always possible. But what should they do with him? Fighting against him, even defeating him in battle, was one thing but killing a king was quite another. England, like most countries in Europe, was a monarchy; how would it be ruled if there was no king?

Cromwell put Charles on trial. Even then many feared the worst. The Parliamentary general, Fairfax, failed to appear at the trial. The court president, John Bradshaw, wore a reinforced hat in case he was attacked (Source 4).

SOURCE 1

Painting of the execution of Charles, January 1649. The four small pictures show: top left, Charles; bottom left, Charles walking to his execution; top right, the executioner holding up Charles's head; bottom right, people dipping their handkerchiefs in his blood.

SEARCHING FOR A SETTLEMENT

The king's execution

The charges against Charles were that he had tried to rule on his own and ignore the laws. He was charged with treason and complete responsibility for the war (see Source 2).

Charles refused to accept that the court had any right to try him. He pointed out that he was the rightful king and so could not be accused of treason, which means attacking the king (see Source 3).

There was never any doubt about the court's verdict. Charles was found guilty and his death warrant signed by 59 of his 135 judges. He was executed on 30 January 1649. As the poet Andrew Marvell wrote:

'He nothing common did or mean
Upon that memorable scene.'

His execution was greeted by the crowd not with a cheer but with a groan. Several people soaked their handkerchiefs in his blood. These bloody handkerchiefs were later said to have caused miraculous cures from illnesses. Royalism was obviously not dead.

The country now had to face two serious questions:
- Who had the right to rule?
- Who had the power to rule?

The next 65 years were to see several different answers to both these questions.

> 'Charles Stuart, King of England, trusted to govern according to the laws of the land, had a wicked design to create for himself an unlimited power to rule according to his will and to overthrow the rights and liberties of the people. To do this he treacherously waged a war against Parliament and the people. He is thus responsible for all the treasons, murders, rapings, burnings, damage and desolation caused during the wars. He is therefore a TYRANT, traitor and murderer.'

SOURCE 2
The charge against King Charles at his trial in January 1649.

> I wish to know by what power I am brought here – I would know by what lawful authority. Remember I am your king, your lawful king . . . I say think well upon it . . . I have a trust committed to me by God, by old and lawful descent. I will not betray it to a new and unlawful authority.

SOURCE 3
Charles's criticism of the court which was putting him on trial, 1649.

SOURCE 4
Metal hat worn by John Bradshaw, president of the court.

Discuss these questions in your groups.

1. Do you agree that Charles was
   a. 'a man of blood', guilty of treason (Source 2), or
   b. a king who could not be put on trial (Source 3)?

2. 135 MPs and army officers were appointed as judges. Many did not turn up; 70 declared him guilty and only 59 signed Charles's death warrant. Why do you think this was?

3. Why did the execution of Charles pose problems for the country?

SEARCHING FOR A SETTLEMENT

The House of Commons

THE RIGHT TO RULE
Parliament, MPs, have the RIGHT TO RULE because they have been chosen by the people in an election.

Saddam Hussein ruler of Iraq, 1991

THE POWER TO RULE
In some countries the army has taken over without an election. They have the POWER TO RULE by force as no one can stop them.

The French Revolution, 1789

REVOLUTION
In a revolution old ideas of who has the right to rule are thrown out as the people seize power for themselves.

England without a king 1649 to 1660

As you can see from the diagram above, the people who have the right to rule are not always the same as the people who have the power to rule. What was the situation in England after 1649?

The power to rule

This clearly lay with the army and its hero leader, Oliver Cromwell, see Source 5. There was no chance of the army giving up power. There was still the danger of a Royalist uprising. There was also a new danger to those in power: revolutionary ideas from groups like the Levellers and the Diggers, who wanted the ordinary people to take over and farm common land. (For more on these ideas, see pages 50 to 51.) Yet people hated the army and the huge cost of keeping it.

The right to rule

Apart from the King, the right to rule lay with the remains (the 'rump') of the last properly elected Parliament, elected back in 1640. Less the half the MPs were left, as all who had fought for the King were excluded, so it was called 'the Rump Parliament'.

SOURCE 5
Oliver Cromwell in 1656.

SEARCHING FOR A SETTLEMENT

SOURCE 6
Whitelocke's account of the end of the Rump Parliament.

'Parliament sitting as usual, the Lord General Cromwell came into the House, dressed in plain clothes with grey worsted stockings. After a while he got up, took his hat off, and spoke of the good things Parliament had done. Then he put his hat on and began pacing the floor of the House, and severely told off the members. After this he said to Colonel Harrison (who was a member of the House), "Call them in". Twenty or thirty musketeers entered. Then the Lord General, pointing to the Speaker in his chair, said to Harrison, "Fetch him down".... Then the Lord General went to the table where the mace lay, which used to be carried before the Speaker, and said, "Take away these baubles". So the soldiers took away the mace and all the House went out. The House was locked and the key with the mace was carried away.'

'Under my rule the people know protection and peace; without me they would truly drown in blood.'

SOURCE 7
Oliver Cromwell speaking in 1657.

Cromwell's search for a settlement

By 1653 Cromwell lost patience with the Rump: it was not doing the things he expected it to do so he dismissed it, see Source 6.

The Barebones Parliament 1653 to 1654
Cromwell and the army now chose 140 MPs whom they trusted. These included a London leather-seller called Praise-God Barebones. However, they talked too much and did nothing, so Cromwell dismissed them.

The Major-Generals 1654 to 1657
Cromwell now became Lord Protector and ruled with one of his major-generals in charge of each region. This was highly unpopular. These men had no right to rule, just the power of the army behind them.

Cromwell as king?
To many people the only way of combining the right to rule with the power to rule was to have a king. In 1657 Cromwell was offered the crown. After much hesitation he refused. You can read his reply to his critics in Source 7.

Restoration 1660
Cromwell died in 1658. His son Richard could not command the respect his father had, and resigned in 1659. There was confusion for nearly a year until General Monck and his army marched to London, took control and invited Charles I's son to come back as Charles II.

ACTIVITY

Get into groups of four. You are all from Parliament's side:

1 A Puritan soldier in the New Model Army. You have had friends killed by Charles's soldiers in battle. You trust Oliver Cromwell who seems to promote people on their merits, and you support the Levellers.

2 A rich merchant who opposed the King in 1640, but felt that Parliament had gone too far by 1642. You are worried by the power of the army and the ideas of people like the soldier, Number 1.

3 A landowner who supported Parliament in the Civil War, but felt it was wrong to execute the king.

4 A shopkeeper who finds that the disruption caused by the Civil War makes business difficult.

You must discuss among yourselves to reach a decision on who should rule England, and how. The discussion takes place:
a in 1649, after the death of Charles,
b in 1658, after the death of Oliver Cromwell.

MAKING CONNECTIONS

The world turned upside down

> 'Day labourers, shopkeepers which have no land of their own, smallholders and craftsmen have no voice in our Commonwealth and no account is made of them but to be ruled.'

SOURCE 8
From Sir Thomas Smith's *Description of England*, 1565 (adapted).

> We desire to share in the freedoms of the state. Have we not an equal interest with the men of this nation? Are our lives, rights or goods to be taken from us more than from men?

SOURCE 9
Women's petition to Parliament, 1649.

Source 8 makes clear that the ordinary people of England, like the labourers described on page 27, had no power. They could not vote, they were often desperately poor, with no land of their own. When they went to church, the priest told them that God had made them poor and they had to accept it. They were not allowed to hold religious ideas of their own.

Then came the Civil War. To win it, Parliament had called on ordinary people to fight for them. As these ordinary soldiers marched all over the country, they had a chance to see different places and exchange views with different people. After the king was defeated, would these soldiers be prepared to go back to their homes and live just as they had done before the war? Thousands of PAMPHLETS and songsheets were published, putting forward revolutionary ideas. At the time they talked of 'a world turned upside down'.

Equality and freedom

Ordinary people wanted to see certain changes that would change their lives for the better.

Religious freedom: people felt they should be allowed to believe what they wanted and to worship freely. Hundreds of religious groups, called sects, were formed. They ran their own chapels and paid their own preachers. For example, 'Fifth Monarchists' believed that Christ was about to return to earth and set up his kingdom here, replacing all earthly rulers. Quakers believed that God was inside everyone, whatever their status. They refused to call people of higher rank 'my lady' or 'sir', or to take their hats off to them, as was the custom.

Political freedom: a group called the Levellers wanted every adult male to have the right to vote (except for servants, beggars or Royalists). In 1647 regiments of the New Model Army elected their own representatives, called 'agitators'. (This was similar to what happened in the Russian army in 1917.) They wore a red ribbon badge and collected 4 pence (half a day's wages) from each soldier for their expenses. They met army leaders and held debates at Putney about further revolutionary changes in the way England was run. Among the other things they called for was the use of English, not Latin, in the law courts, and education for all. Women also petitioned Parliament for equality, see Source 9.

Economic equality: in many revolutions the poor look at the wealth of the rich and call for more equality. The 1640s and 1650s were hard times, with bad harvests. Many demanded fair shares in the country's wealth, see Source 10. The Diggers claimed that poor people should take over the common land and farm it together, see Source 11. One such commune was set up at St George's Hill in Surrey and others were begun elsewhere.

> 'The great things that have been done for Parliament have been done by the meaner sort of men. It was unconscionable [unjust] to the poorer sort of people that one should have £10,000 and another more deserving and useful should not be worth 2d.'

SOURCE 10
William Walwyn, a Leveller, writing in 1646.

MAKING CONNECTIONS

> The power now is in your hands, the nation's representatives. Oh let the first thing you do be this: to set the land free! Let the gentry have their enclosed fields and let the common people have their commons and waste land to themselves. The poorest man hath as just a right to land as the richest man . . . true freedom lies in the free enjoyment of the earth.

SOURCE 11
Extract from a pamphlet written by Gerard Winstanley appealing to Parliament, 1649. Winstanley was the leader of the Diggers.

SOURCE 12
Burford Church, Oxfordshire.

SOURCE 13
The Declaration of Independence of the USA was signed in 1776. It began 'we hold these truths to be self evident, that all men are created equal'.

1 What did each of these groups want:
   Fifth Monarchists?
   Levellers?
   Diggers?

2 What did all three groups have in common?

3 Why did the Civil War bring out these ideas?

4 What is the link between these ideas and the French Revolution?

The Revolution crushed

The Levellers in the army failed to get what they wanted and when they mutinied in 1649 their leaders were rounded up and shot in the churchyard at Burford, see Source 12. Local landlords burnt the Digger communes after a few months. After 1660 the old order returned in strength. Bishops were restored. Women were put back in their old place, that is, owing obedience to men. Wandering preachers went back to their normal jobs.

But it was not the end of the Levellers' ideas. Some rebels emigrated to America, hoping to set up the kind of society and government they wanted there. But even in America, these rebel emigrants and their descendants found they were not free. America was still a colony, ruled from Europe. Increasingly, Americans resented this. They wanted to run their new country in their own way. In 1776, the leaders of the 13 British colonies in America declared themselves independent. As you can see from Source 13, the idea of equality became the foundation of their new nation.

The Americans' Declaration of Independence led to bitter war. Britain did not want to give up its rich colonies. The American rebels were helped by soldiers from Europe, especially from France, where many people were inspired by new, radical ideas (see pages 70 to 71). They saw the rebels as freedom-fighters, struggling to achieve a better style of government. Soon they would be trying to apply these ideas in France itself.

SEARCHING FOR A SETTLEMENT

SOURCE 14
The coronation procession of King Charles II.

The return of the monarchy

To all Royalists, and to many who weren't, by 1660 the only answer to the question 'who had the right to rule?' was King Charles II. He was given a tremendous welcome on his return to England and a splendid coronation (see Source 14). Parliament granted him an income of £1,200,000, far more than Charles I had managed on in the 1630s. He seemed therefore to have the power, as well as the right, to rule.

Real power after 1660, however, lay with the rich landowners who now controlled Parliament. They had been horrified by the democratic ideas and freedom of worship of the 1640s and 1650s. They were resentful of the people of lower social class who had ruled the country in those years. They hated the very name of Oliver Cromwell, and had his dead body dug up and hanged. Those people still alive in England who had signed Charles I's death warrant were arrested and executed. The old prayer book was restored and 1,760 ministers who refused to accept it were removed from the Church of England. In 1664 religious worship outside the Church of England was banned. Members of Puritan groups, such as the Quakers, who had flourished under Oliver Cromwell were fined and imprisoned.

Parliament believed in the monarchy, and thought the upheavals were over. But no one could wipe away history: Charles I had been opposed, defeated and executed; Charles II had been invited to become king. MPs might not have agreed with the idea, but a king could clearly be un-made as well as made. By 1688 MPs had to face this, because the king was doing the one thing which turned the country against him.

SOURCE 15
King James II.

SEARCHING FOR A SETTLEMENT

James II

We have already seen that by the 17th century most people were violently anti-Roman Catholic. Some idea of the strength of feeling can be seen in Source 16. Charles II died in 1685, becoming a Roman Catholic on his deathbed. His brother James (Source 15), who became James II, was already a Roman Catholic.

The laws said that only members of the Church of England could hold important jobs. Kings could remove laws in certain cases and James began to do this to put Roman Catholics into the army, universities and local government. He also got his supporters elected to Parliament (Source 17).

James's heir was his daughter Mary, who was Protestant and married to his Protestant nephew William of Orange. Many people were worried and angry about James's Roman Catholic views, but felt the future was safe. Then his new Roman Catholic wife gave birth to a son. Secret contacts had been made with William and in November 1688 he arrived in England (Source 18). As he slowly made his way from Devon to London, James's supporters slipped away to join him. James fled to France and William and Mary became joint monarchs as William III and Mary II.

> Having been called by Almighty God to rule these kingdoms, I think of nothing but the spread of the Catholic religion. This is the true service of God for which I am willing to sacrifice everything.

SOURCE 17
James II's religious views.

> 'Imagine you see troops of Papists ravishing your wives and daughters and plundering your houses. Casting your eye towards Smithfield imagine you see your father or your mother or some of your nearest and dearest relations tied to a stake in the midst of flames – this was a frequent spectacle the last time Papacy reigned among us.'

SOURCE 16
Extract from an anti-Roman Catholic pamphlet of 1679.

SOURCE 18
William of Orange landing at Brixham, Devon, 5 November 1688.

Discuss your answers to these questions in pairs or small groups.

1 The events described in Source 16 did not actually happen in 1679. What is its use as a piece of evidence about the 1670s?

2 Why do you think William landed in Devon, far away from London, the centre of power?

SEARCHING FOR A SETTLEMENT

The Glorious Revolution

The extraordinary events of 1688 and 1689 have been called the 'Bloodless Revolution' or the 'Glorious Revolution'. Are these good names for what happened?

The take-over of the throne by William and Mary was bloodless in England and Wales but not in Scotland or, as we shall see, in Ireland. It was only a revolution at the top. The monarch changed, but there was no change in the people who held power (see Source 19). These were the rich landowners who controlled Parliament. There was no change in this situation for 150 years. For them it was indeed a 'Glorious Revolution'.

The Settlement

In 1689, and over the next few years, relations between monarchs and Parliament were settled, leaving monarchs in much the same position as they hold now.

- No monarch could be a Roman Catholic.
- Only Parliament could pass laws and monarchs could not dispense with them as James II had done.
- People were allowed to worship freely. This excluded Roman Catholics and all universities and government jobs were still reserved for members of the Church of England. Nevertheless, Quakers and other groups were able to build chapels or meeting houses of their own (see Source 20).
- Parliamentary elections had to be held at least every three years.

'For both the Protestant religion and the laws and liberties of the nation. Our expectation is intended for no other design but to have a free and lawful Parliament assembled as soon as possible.'

SOURCE 19
From William's Declaration of why he had landed in England, 1688

William brought England into the war against France he had been fighting since 1686. The war was almost permanent, going on from 1689 to 1697 and 1702 to 1713. This was very expensive: the army alone cost £2.7 million a year. William could not keep asking Parliament for money, so they came to an arrangement:

- Parliament would take over the cost of the army, raising money from taxes.
- Parliament had the right to decide foreign policy.
- The monarch was given an income from the Civil List.

SOURCE 20
Long Sutton Quaker meeting house, Somerset, built in 1707.

SEARCHING FOR A SETTLEMENT

SOURCE 21
Queen Anne in the House of Lords.

SOURCE 22
The Union Flag, formed from the flags of England, Scotland and Ireland.

The Act of Union 1707

William and Mary had no children. Their successor, Mary's sister Anne, had 17 babies, all of whom died young. The English Parliament looked to the rulers of Hanover in Germany, descendants of James I, to become monarchs after Anne (see family tree on page 6). Scotland, however, was still a separate country. Oliver Cromwell had united the two for a brief period (1652 to 1660) after he had defeated the Scots. Now the Scots demanded the right to choose their own ruler. Many Scots were loyal to the Stuarts, and wanted James II's son to rule. This could bring Scotland into the wars on France's side.

This was unthinkable to the English, so an Act of Union was passed in 1707 on terms which the Scots could agree. 45 Scottish MPs and 16 Scottish peers entered Parliament. They kept their own Church, law and education but could trade on the same terms as English merchants. The United Kingdom of England, Scotland, Ireland and Wales was formed.

---

attainment target

These questions are about people's attitudes and motives during the events described in these pages.

1. Why did so many people leave James and join William as he made his way from Brixham to London?
2. Why did William make the promises in Source 19?
3. Many people after 1660 thought that monarchs should always be obeyed completely. How would they react to the events of 1688?
4. Why did Parliament want regular elections?
5. Why did William and Mary accept all the limitations on their power listed opposite?

SOURCE 23
Map of Ireland.

SOURCE 24
An illustration of 1575 showing a woman from the Pale and a Gaelic Irishman.

> An old woman, which was his foster-mother, took up his head when he was quartered, and sucked up all the blood running thereout, saying that the earth was not worthy to drink it.

SOURCE 25
The poet Edmund Spenser, secretary to Queen Elizabeth's representative in Ireland, describes the execution of Murrough O'Brien in 1583. O'Brien was hanged, drawn and quartered by the English. That is he was first hanged, and while still alive, his insides were cut out and then his body cut into four parts.

Ireland in 1500

English monarchs had called themselves Kings of Ireland ever since 1155. However, the only part of Ireland which they really controlled at the end of the Middle Ages was an area around Dublin called 'the Pale' (see Source 23). 'Beyond the Pale' lords and chiefs ruled like little kings. Some of these lords were descended from Norman barons who had taken land in Ireland in the 12th century. Others, like the rest of the people, were Gaelic, with their own language, poetry, laws and customs. Warfare between the chiefs was common. This made a settled farming life very difficult for ordinary people. They grew some crops, but mostly kept huge herds of cattle, which grazed on the move over a wide area.

A vicious circle

The English did not understand the Irish: because they were different, the English regarded them as uncivilised. This can be seen in Source 24, where the Irishman is shown as a wild savage. In Source 25, Spenser obviously thought the old woman's action was barbaric, but that hanging, drawing and quartering was not.

Religion helped to turn this mistrust into hatred. When England became Protestant, Ireland stayed firmly Roman Catholic. The Bible and Prayer Book in English meant nothing to the Gaelic-speaking people. In Queen Elizabeth's reign, the Pope told the Irish that they did not have to obey their English rulers. Irish rebellions now posed a new danger to England in their war with Catholic Spain. Spanish forces helped the rebels and so might gain a base close to England. There were four Irish rebellions in Elizabeth's reign, and her government had to send large armies to put them down. Many Irish were killed.

Plantations

The English came up with a solution to their Irish 'problem'. The Irish people, they thought, were uncivilised, Roman Catholic rebels, so should be

SEARCHING FOR A SETTLEMENT

replaced by civilised, Protestant English settlers. Land was taken from the Irish and handed out to English or Scottish farming families as 'plantations'. About ten settler families were 'planted' on each 1,000 acres (see Source 27). These settlers introduced English farming methods, sold off the cattle, and grew crops. The Irish were employed as labourers on the land they had once used themselves. In 1603, Roman Catholics owned 90% of Ireland. By 1641 they owned only 59%.

So a vicious circle of hatred grew up (see Source 26). There was brutality on both sides. English settlers would only go to Ireland if they felt safe, so Irish opposition was harshly crushed. When the Irish did rise up in protest in 1641, they attacked English settlers and 2,000 were MASSACRED (see Source 28).

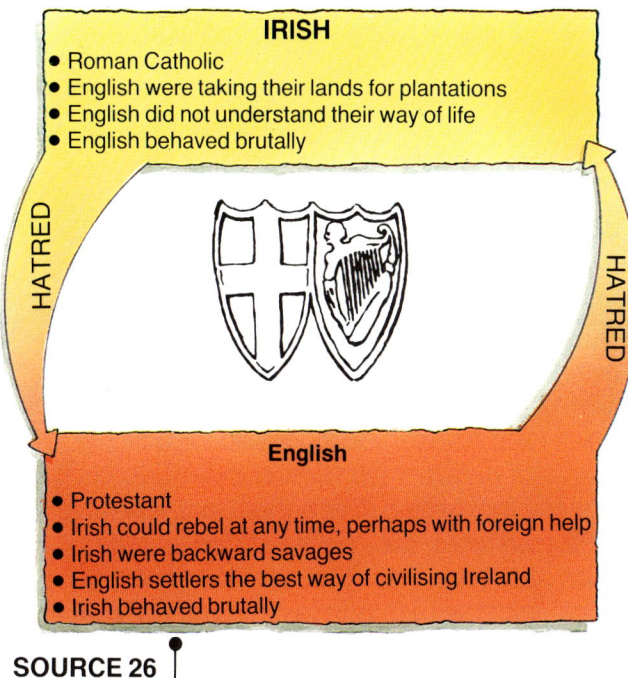

SOURCE 26
The 'vicious circle'.

IRISH
- Roman Catholic
- English were taking their lands for plantations
- English did not understand their way of life
- English behaved brutally

English
- Protestant
- Irish could rebel at any time, perhaps with foreign help
- Irish were backward savages
- English settlers the best way of civilising Ireland
- Irish behaved brutally

SOURCE 27
The Vintners' Settlement at Bellaghy, Ulster, 1622.

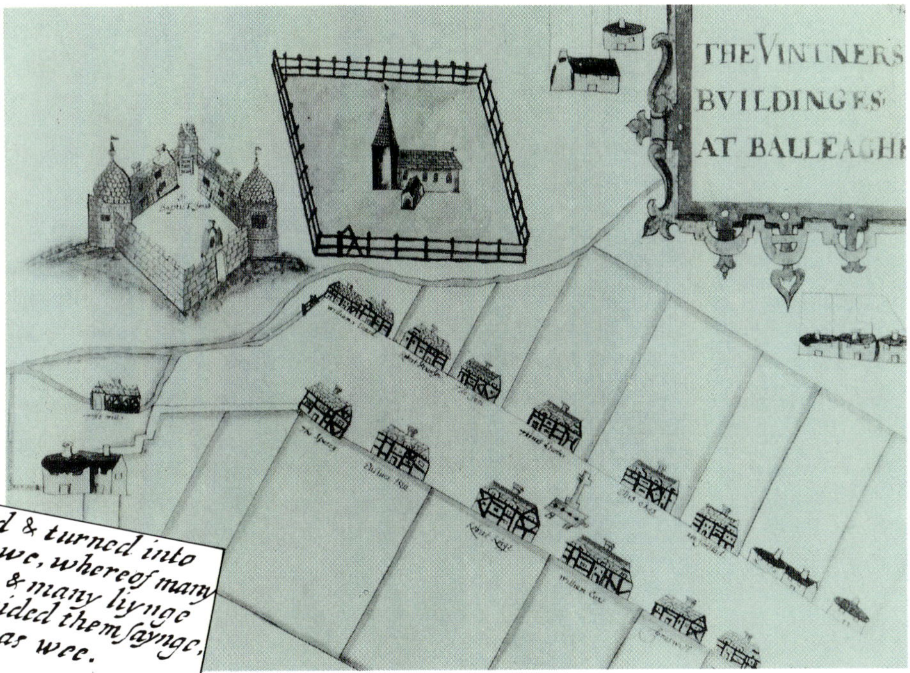

SOURCE 28
A Protestant view of the Irish rebels of 1641.

English Protestants stripd naked & turned into the mountaines in the frost, & snowe, whereof many hundreds are perished to death, & many lynge dead in diches & sauages upbraided them saynge, now are ye wilde Irish as well as wee.

1. In Source 27 find: the castle, to defend the settlers; the new Protestant church; the two-storey settlers' houses along the street; their gardens; the stocks by the town cross; the watermill; huts for the native Irish.

2. What does Source 24 tell us about how the English felt about the Irish?

3. In what ways does Source 28 try to stir up hatred against Irish Roman Catholics?

SEARCHING FOR A SETTLEMENT

Cromwell and Ireland

Pictures such as Source 28 horrified Protestants in England. As soon as the Civil War was won, Oliver Cromwell went to Ireland. He wanted revenge for the massacres of 1641, and permanent peace for Ireland. For him, permanent peace meant expelling all priests and rebels, taking most of the land away from Roman Catholics, and trying to convert the Irish to Protestantism. As we have seen (see page 45), Cromwell was tolerant towards different Protestant views, but Source 29 makes clear his attitude to Roman Catholics.

Most of his army felt the same (see Source 30). After the Irish rebels in Drogheda and Wexford had surrendered, they were all killed and the towns SACKED. Roman Catholic landowners were driven from their lands in Ulster, Munster and Leinster and bundled on to poor land west of the River Shannon. Thousands of acres of land were given to Protestant settlers. A strip of land, four miles wide, along the River Shannon, was given to Protestant soldier-settlers. By 1665, only 22% of Ireland was in Roman Catholic hands, mostly in Connacht.

But Cromwell's plans to convert the Irish to Protestantism failed. Ireland therefore now had Protestant, English-speaking landowners dominating Roman Catholic, Gaelic-speaking peasants.

> I meddle not with any man's conscience, but if by liberty of conscience you mean a liberty to exercise the Mass [the Roman Catholic service] I judge it best to use plain dealing and to let you know . . . that will not be allowed of.

SOURCE 29
In 1650 Oliver Cromwell was asked by an Irish Roman Catholic that people should be allowed to worship according to their own beliefs (their conscience). This was his reply.

SOURCE 30
St George, dressed as a Cromwellian soldier, trampling on the Irish dragon, 1649.

The battle of the Boyne, July 1690

When the Roman Catholic James II fled from England in 1689 he went to the one part of his kingdom which would support him: Roman Catholic Ireland. The Irish soon formed an army for him. Protestants in Ireland feared a repeat of 1641, and took refuge in towns, such as Derry, which were beseiged.

William of Orange, King William III, arrived in Ireland with a combined English and Dutch army. To him, this was just part of his long war with James's allies, the French. The Pope had quarrelled with the French and in fact supported William. His forces defeated James at the battle of the Boyne in July 1690 (see Source 31). The Irish went on to fight other battles, but peace was made in 1691.

The Protestant victory

After William's victory the Protestants in Ireland made sure their control was complete. Roman Catholics were banned from Parliament, the law, university and the navy. They could not vote, run a

SEARCHING FOR A SETTLEMENT

SOURCE 31
A contemporary picture of King William III at the battle of the Boyne. William is on horseback at the centre of the group of horsemen in the bottom right-hand corner.

SOURCE 32
'King Billy', a modern painting on a wall in Belfast.

school, or own a horse worth more than £5. Roman Catholic bishops were BANISHED and could be hanged, drawn and quartered if they returned. Only a few registered priests were allowed. Roman Catholics found it difficult to inherit land and the amount they had fell to 14% by 1703, 5% by 1776.

The battle of the Boyne was thus very important to Protestants. To this day pictures of 'King Billy' can be seen on walls and banners in Protestant parts of Northern Ireland (Source 32).

attainment target

1. 'In the 17th century the English treated the Irish badly.' Is this statement a fact or a point of view?

2. What do you think about the way the English ruled in Ireland in this period? Which out of Sources 23 to 32 would you use to support your interpretation?

3. Compare Sources 31 and 32. The Ulster Protestant who painted Source 32 saw William as a Protestant hero protecting Ireland from the Pope and Roman Catholics. What facts does this view of William seem to ignore?

4. Why do you think the battle of the Boyne is seen as such an important event in Irish history?

MAKING CONNECTIONS

SOURCE 34 Stourhead House, Wiltshire.

SOURCE 33 Henry Hoare, the banker who had Stourhead House built.

Winners and losers

After all the battles, bloodshed and crises of the 17th century, who won? It was not the monarchy. As you saw on pages 53 and 55, monarchs were invited to take the crown in 1688 and again in 1714. They were served with dignity and lived in luxury, but they had nothing like the power of 17th century monarchs. Nor was it the common people. The hopes of the Levellers, the Diggers and others in the 1640s that Britain would become a real democracy and that there would be real equality were dashed.

The real winners, those who ruled Britain in the 18th and early 19th centuries, were the great landowners – the 'magnates'. They were the people who had offered the crown to William and Mary in 1688 and George I in 1714. They owned huge estates, they were the king's ministers, they ran Parliament, trade, and their local counties. Typically, they were people like Henry Hoare, Source 33. His grandfather was a London horse-dealer, but his father, Sir Richard Hoare, was a goldsmith who became a banker. Henry went into banking but also bought large estates in Wiltshire. He had Stourhead House built in 1722 (Source 34). It was designed in the Palladian style by Colen Campbell. Houses built in the Palladian style expressed power, balance, control, calm. They were the houses of the ruling classes. Unlike Montacute and Hardwick, see pages 20 and 28, they were symmetrical inside as well as outside, with grand rooms for entertaining. Unlike the two Elizabethan houses, where servants sat around in the entrance hall and used the same stairs as everyone else, the servants at Stourhead were confined to the basement and moved around the house using special backstairs. Bess of Hardwick (page 28) only had six books; the Hoares had a music room and later added a library and art gallery in 1792.

MAKING CONNECTIONS

Power struggles in France

In France power was held quite differently: in the hands of the king. He governed with the help of royal ministers, chosen, paid – and dismissed at will – by him. France did have a sort of parliament (called the Estates-General), made up of representatives from different groups in society. (You can read more about it on page 74.) But French kings refused to summon it after 1614. They preferred to rule alone.

An awful warning

King Charles I of England had been married to Louis XIII's sister. His oldest son, later King Charles II, had taken refuge at the French court during the English Civil War. So King Louis XIV of France (ruled 1643 to 1715) was well aware of the dangers that lay in wait for kings who lost the goodwill of their most powerful subjects, or let control of the government slip from their hands.

Versailles

But Louis was determined to avoid execution. Instead, he decided to impress everyone with his royal splendour, power and strength. He built a vast, magnificent palace at Versailles, about 16 kilometres outside Paris (Source 35). Paris was the capital city of France, where the Estates-General and important law courts met, and where noble families and rich lawyers maintained fine town houses (called 'hotels').

The centre of royal power

Versailles was almost a whole day's journey (by horse-drawn coach) from Paris. But now anyone – however rich or important – had to leave Paris and travel there if they wanted to find favour with the king, to offer him advice or to ask for his help. All government jobs also came from Versailles. They were handed out by the king and his ministers to courtiers who waited anxiously in one of the grand 'presence' chambers for a formal audience. Often, petitioners had to stay at the palace for weeks in smelly, dirty rooms. But a meeting with the king was so important that even a share in one of these back bedrooms was a sign that you were in touch with royal power.

SOURCE 35
The Palace of Versailles seen from its elegant gardens.

THE FRENCH REVOLUTION

Europe in 1789

The French Revolution marked a major turning point for France. After 1789, life would never be the same for French men and women, whether they were rich or poor. As you read through these units and study the sources, you can find out how people reacted to the events of the Revolution, in France and in neighbouring lands. You can discover how the changes that took place during the Revolution and the Napoleonic era have shaped present-day France. You can also see how the ideals of liberty and equality, which inspired the Revolution, have encouraged revolutions in many other countries over the past 200 years, and are still influential today.

THE FRENCH REVOLUTION

ANCIEN REGIME (royal rule)

1780

1787 Financial crisis, widespread discontent.

1788 Bad harvests and food shortages. Decision to call Estates-General.

1789 Famine and riots. Attack on the Bastille by mobs. The Revolution begins. Declaration of the Rights of Man and the Citizen.

REVOLUTIONARY ASSEMBLIES

1791 The royal family tries to escape.

1792 Monarchy abolished. A republic declared.

1793 Louis XVI executed.

THE TERROR

Jacobin faction seizes power. Terror begins.

1794 Robespierre executed – the end of the Terror.

THE DIRECTORY

1795 Directory (committee of moderate politicians) now rules France.

1796 Napoleon's first victories in battle.

NAPOLEON'S RULE

1799 Napoleon seizes power.

1804 Napoleon becomes Emperor
– reforms French government.
– starts to conquer vast empire.

1812 Napoleon defeated in Russia.

NEW MONARCHY

1814 Louis XVIII becomes king.

1815 France defeated at battle of Waterloo. Napoleon sent into exile. France governed by a King again.

1821 Napoleon dies in exile.

UNIT 5

Land and people

France in the 18th century

Eighteenth century France was a big country compared with other countries in Europe. As you can see from Source 1, the French government ruled over an area twice the size of England and Wales, and almost ten times the size of Switzerland.

In the early 18th century, there were around 20 million French people. However, by the time the French Revolution began in 1789, there were probably at least 26 million.

France was made up of what had been small, independent nations. These had been brought under French control during the 15th and 16th centuries. French peasants therefore spoke different local languages, lived in different styles of houses, and grew different kinds of crops. They even had different faiths: most were Catholics, but some were Protestants. Their daily lives were governed by a confusing number of ancient local laws.

AIMS

In this unit we look at France in the years before the outbreak of the French Revolution, from around 1770 to 1789. We learn how French society was organised, how the economy was run and how the country was governed. What was life like for the people of France at this time?

As we study pre-revolutionary France, can we see any conflicts or tensions within society that might help us to suggest why the Revolution broke out?

SOURCE 1
France in the 18th century.

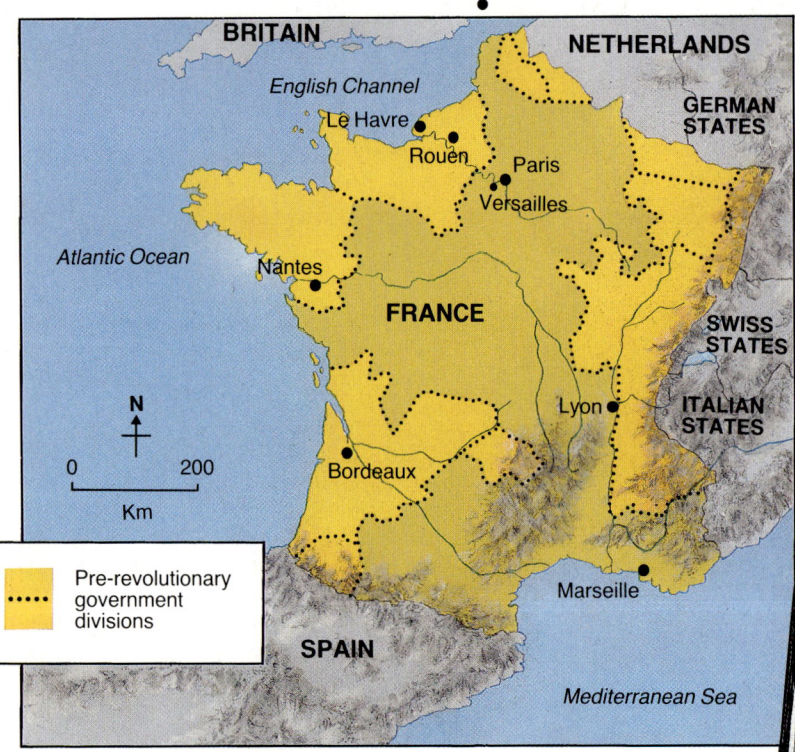

Pre-revolutionary government divisions

SOURCE 2
How one 18th century French artist saw peasant life. The original caption reads 'Born for hard work and suffering.'

LAND AND PEOPLE

SOURCE 3
Traditional farmland in Central France today.

'All the country girls and women are without shoes and stockings; and the ploughmen at work have neither *sabots* (clogs) nor stockings to their feet. This is a poverty that strikes at the root of national prosperity.'

SOURCE 4
Written by Arthur Young, an English traveller in France, 10 June 1787.

Peasants

Almost all of these people were peasants earning a living from the land, but this did not make them equal. Their income varied greatly, depending on how much land they farmed, and who it belonged to (see Source 3).

The wealthiest peasants were called LABOUREURS. They owned or rented large farms, and produced enough food to feed their families and still have a surplus to sell. Next came MÉTAYERS who leased fields from landlords, and were provided with tools, seeds and livestock. In return, the *métayers* gave the landlords at least half of what they produced every year. The rest struggled to feed their families from the land they rented. Often, they had to take on other work to make extra money, or leave their homes for part of the year to search for work in the towns. Others became beggars.

Poverty and taxes

Almost all these peasants, except the *laboureurs*, were extremely poor (see Sources 2 and 4). Their hardships were increased by the taxes they had to pay. Unlike other groups in society (see page 73) they had not found a way of avoiding them.

1. Although many peasants were poor, they did not protest or rebel. Suggest two reasons for this.
2. If you were a peasant who wanted to improve your life, what would you do?

The typical tax bill of a peasant family each year might include:
- TAILLE PERSONELLE – a yearly tax on possessions
- CAPITATION – poll tax
- VINGTIÈME – a tax of one-twentieth on land
- TITHE – a tax on produce, paid to the Church.

Almost everyone in France also paid:
- GABELLE – a tax on salt
- DOUANES – customs duties on goods moved to market.

Peasants also had to pay ancient FEUDAL DUES such as paying the local lord to use his mill to grind their corn, or his oven to bake their bread. By the 18th century, the nobles who had inherited the rights to collect these dues had usually 'sold' them to wealthy businessmen or to *laboureurs*. It was always the poor peasants who ended up paying, as Source 5 shows.

SOURCE 5
Pre-revolutionary cartoon, complaining about the burden of taxation carried by the peasants.

Nobles, bourgeoisie and clergy

Peasants made up the largest section of French society – about 80 per cent. We can divide the others into three separate groups: nobles, BOURGEOIS and clergy.

The nobles

Traditionally, nobles were identified as men and women with titles – dukes, duchesses etc – who had noble ANCESTORS. They could trace their families back for many generations, to men who fought alongside kings in far-off medieval times.

By the 18th century, this ancient definition of nobility was very out of date. Many of the old noble families had died out, or had lost their wealth and influence (see Source 6). Their place had been taken by men who had been given lands and a title as a reward for government service – acting as royal ministers – or for duties in the local PARLEMENTS (law courts), which played an important part in French political life. These 'new' nobles were often lawyers. Divisions between 'old' and 'new' nobles were gradually dying out. All that mattered was riches, a title, and political power. Nobles who had achieved these things built magnificent stately homes and commemorated their success in elegant family portraits, like the group in Source 7.

The bourgeoisie

BOURGEOISIE means 'town-dwellers'. The bourgeoisie in 18th century France was made up of merchants, craft-workers, factory-owners, doctors, teachers, journalists, writers and artists. There were lawyers, who worked as government officials, and a great many shopkeepers. There were also servants, unemployed peasants (see Source 8) and beggars.

Trade and prosperity

French towns prospered during the 18th century. Successful members of the bourgeoisie had plenty of money, earned through trade, from government positions, or in professional fees. Nobles, bourgeoisie and clergy played an important part in government (see Source 9). They also spent a lot of money on enjoying themselves (see Source 10).

> 'They allow their country houses to go to decay ... and reside in dark holes in the Upper Town ... without light, air or convenience. There they starve within doors, that they may have the wherewithall to purchase fine clothes and appear (in public) dressed once a day ...'

SOURCE 6
Description of impoverished nobles' lifestyle written by an Irishman, Tobias Smollett, in 1763.

SOURCE 8
Political cartoon: 'The awakening of the Third Estate', showing a nobleman, a priest and a peasant all in ceremonial dress.

SOURCE 7
Not all nobles were as wealthy as the Duc de Penthièvres, shown here with his wife and family.

LAND AND PEOPLE

KING

- head of state – in charge of policy for war and peace
- made new laws and was chief judge
- appointed national and local government officials
- raised taxes and controlled currency
- had duty to:
  – uphold privileges of PARLEMENTS
  – respect the law
  – summon ESTATES-GENERAL to raise new taxes

PARLEMENTS

- ancient local law courts – tried criminals
- members: nobles and well-educated bourgeois
- debated and accepted all new royal laws
- could be overruled by KING
- often quarrelled with KING

ESTATES-GENERAL

- assembly of representatives elected by:
  1st Estate – clergy
  2nd Estate – nobles
  3rd Estate – everyone else
- expressed public opinion
- authorised new taxes when KING asked for them
- had not met since 1614

SOURCE 9
Structure of the French government before the Revolution.

SOURCE 10
Wealthy bourgeois men and women met to walk and talk at public promenades like the Gallery of the Palais Royal, seen here.

These wealthy town-dwellers were usually ambitious. Often, they were richer than the old aristocrats. Arranged marriages between poor noble sons and rich bourgeois daughters were common. Both families would hope to benefit from the deal. As one historian said, 'Not all nobles . . . were rich, but, sooner or later, all the rich ended up noble.'

The clergy

Parish priests played an important part in society, especially in the countryside. Apart from their religious duties, they were often the only educated people in villages, so they sometimes acted as leaders of political opinion as well. Monasteries were also powerful, because they were major landowners. The Church owned 20 per cent of all the land in France. Senior churchmen, such as bishops and abbots, took part in national and international politics. They were often appointed from noble families, and were chosen for their high status and good political connections, rather than their holy lives. You can see one of these 'noble' churchmen standing next to the nobleman in Source 8.

1 Look at Sources 7, 8 and 10. Can you tell, just from these pictures, who was the richest person?

2 Which would you rather have been, a noble, a bourgeois, or a priest?

LAND AND PEOPLE

SOURCE 11
Portrait of King Louis XVI, by Antoine-Francois Callet (1741–1823).

'He is honest and wishes to do good, but has neither genius (intelligence) or education to show the way towards that good which he desires.'

SOURCE 12
Comment by the American ambassador to Louis XVI's court.

'It is in my person alone that sovereign power lives ... It is from me alone that my courts get their authority ... It is to me alone that law-making power belongs ... The whole public order comes from me, ...'

SOURCE 13
Remark made by Louis XV.

SOURCE 14
The royal palace at Versailles, near Paris, where Louis XVI and his family lived. It was the centre of royal government.

Kings and courtiers

King Louis XVI of France came to the throne in 1774, when he was 20 years old. He was a member of the Bourbon DYNASTY which had ruled France since 1589. Source 11 shows a splendid portrait of Louis XVI. The artist has copied the majestic pose and the costume from an earlier portrait of Louis XIV (Louis XVI's great-great grandfather). Louis XVI tried to follow the example set by his glorious ancestor, but found it very difficult indeed.

King Louis XIV had been intelligent, ruthless and determined. Louis XVI was different (see Source 12). He was well-meaning, but shy and not very quick-thinking. Hunting and horse-riding were his great passions. He preferred talking to his grooms (workers in the stables) than to his ministers. He did not know how to handle crafty, ambitious politicians.

A Divine Right to rule?

King Louis XIV believed that God had given him the right to rule. Therefore, his subjects, the French people, should obey him without question. Source 13 shows that later kings followed his example. Louis XVI was brought up to believe in DIVINE RIGHT too. According to this theory, kings ruled with the help of a parliament, called the Estates-General, but this had not met since 1614. Ever since then, kings had governed the country with the help of ministers chosen by themselves.

Many people in France were unhappy with this system of government. The nobles – especially those who served as judges in the local *parlements* – wanted to limit royal power by bringing back their traditional rights. The bourgeoisie felt frustrated by royal government, which was often slow, inefficient and CORRUPT.

LAND AND PEOPLE

SOURCE 16
A 'galante' (elegant, refined and romantic) painting by Antoine Watteau (1684–1721), showing an imaginary party in an enchanted landscape.

SOURCE 15
Comment by the Swedish nobleman Axel von Fersen, a great friend of Marie Antoinette.

> 'We are in a tumult of feasts, delights and all manner of entertainments. . . We never have time to do all arranged for us . . . We have already had a grand opera at Versailles and a State Ball, not to mention very many dinners and suppers. Tomorrow there is a feast in the Queen's large garden at Trianon . . . We miss none of them.'

Life at Versailles

Following another royal tradition, Louis XVI maintained the vast palace of Versailles, shown in Source 14, as a place to entertain the nobility. Noble families came to live there, in the hope of winning a share of royal government and power. Versailles was also a place where gossip, intrigue and glamorous entertainments flourished freely (see Source 15).

During the reign of Louis XV, Versailles had been a great centre of art, music and theatre, encouraged by the King's mistress, Madame de Pompadour. This had won respect for French culture throughout Europe. But now, under Louis XVI, the elegant, GALANTE world pictured in Source 16 was fading away. Louis XVI's queen, Marie Antoinette (see Source 17) was more interested in escaping from the stuffiness of court life, and in light-hearted amusements. In itself, this was harmless, but in political terms it did not give a very good impression of the monarchy. If the Queen and her friends did not take the royal court seriously, who would?

SOURCE 17
Portrait of Queen Marie Antoinette, painted in 1783 by Louise-Elisabeth Vigée-Lebrun (1755–1842).

1. What ideas do you think passed through Louis XVI's mind while his portrait (Source 11) was being painted?
2. What impression of the personality of Louis XVI do you get from these pages?
3. Do you think Louis XVI was an effective king, able to rule the country well and deal with any crisis?

LAND AND PEOPLE

New ideas

The eighteenth century was an exciting time in which to live if you were a writer, a scientist, or anyone interested in new ideas. In England, Isaac Newton was putting forward revolutionary theories about how the universe was made. The philosopher John Locke was suggesting a totally new way of studying human behaviour. In America, Benjamin Franklin was performing daring experiments with electricity. In Russia, Peter the Great had founded an Academy, where brilliant mathematicians could teach.

In France, in 1751, Denis Diderot (Source 18) and Jean d'Alembert began to publish an encyclopedia (Source 19). They aimed to explain all the recent new discoveries in science and technology to the general public, and they succeeded very well. New ideas were also popularised by books such as Buffon's *Natural History*, a scientific listing of animals (see Source 20), and in many French journals.

Scientific criticism

Diderot and d'Alembert were unlike other scientific publishers. They chose to comment on current events and political ideas, as well as on scientific happenings. They even criticised the French King's claim to rule by Divine Right, and many 'unscientific' beliefs taught by the Church.

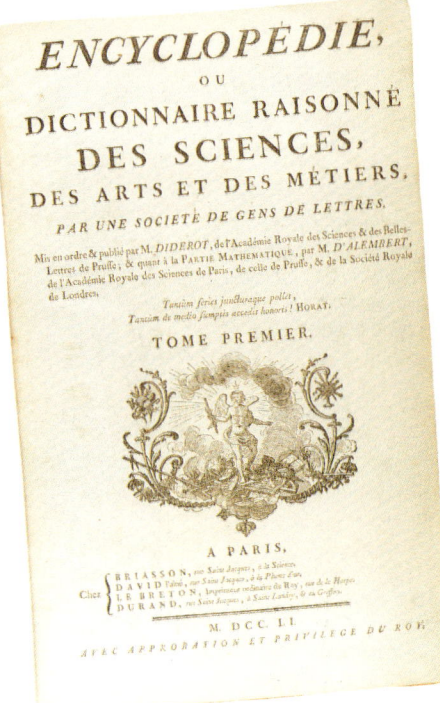

SOURCE 19
Page from the *Encyclopedia*, published by Diderot and d'Alembert, 1751–1786.

SOURCE 20
A spread from Buffon's *Natural History*.

SOURCE 18
Denis Diderot (1713–1784)

attainment target

1. How do you think each of these groups felt about the American revolution: King Louis and his family; peasants; nobles; bourgeois and priests?

2. Explain why each of these people or groups felt this way.

3. Do you think everyone in the groups above felt the same? Explain your answer.

LAND AND PEOPLE

SOURCE 21
The Caveau (Cellar) Café in Paris. People came here to discuss new ideas and to read.

'Humanity... freed from its chains, released from the power of fate and from that of the enemies of progress, advancing with a firm and sure step along the path of truth, virtue and happiness.'

SOURCE 22
A remark made by the philosopher Jean-Jacques Rousseau (1712–1778) describing what he wanted France to be like in future.

Censorship

Diderot and d'Alembert were brave to publish, as the French government punished writers of books they felt were 'damaging to the state'. One leading French scientific thinker, known as Voltaire, was put in prison for composing humorous verses about the royal family which were also very rude. In fact, Voltaire supported royal power but he thought that Louis XVI was not very good at running the government.

The King put people in prison for their writing, but he could not stop people talking. Writers, philosophers and scientists met regularly in cafés (see Source 21) and reading rooms. A new and lively political community was being formed.

Revolution and reform

What sort of ideas did these men discuss? The works of Voltaire were popular, along with the writings of Jean-Jacques Rousseau (see Source 22). After 1775, news of the American Revolution was eagerly waited for. France took America's side in the war against Britain (see Source 23), and many French thinkers were inspired by American ideas. This made some French people look critically at their own society. Perhaps that could also be improved?

However, most people feared change, as Source 24 suggests. They agreed with Montesquieu when he argued that the ideal society should aim at 'a balance of powers'. No single group – royalty, nobles, clergy or bourgeoisie – should be more powerful than the rest. This way of looking at things called for peaceful reform, not violent revolution.

SOURCE 23
Signing the American Declaration of Independence, 1776. This picture was painted in 1819.

SOURCE 24
Comment by an influential French nobleman and philosopher, Charles, Baron de Montesquieu (1689–1755).

'Is it always better to change things than to go on suffering?'

LAND AND PEOPLE

Economic problems

During the 18th century, France was one of the wealthiest and most powerful nations in Europe, largely because of overseas trade (see Source 25). French merchants – wealthy bourgeois and many nobles – invested in plantations in French colonies overseas. The slaves who worked on these plantations were often treated badly, but the merchants did not care. They made high profits by importing valuable tropical goods, especially sugar, cotton, coffee, chocolate, vanilla and spices.

French sea ports on the Atlantic coast, like Dieppe and Le Havre, were rebuilt to cope with the increasing imports. They also profited from the large numbers of slaves brought from Africa to be shipped across the Atlantic.

Elegance and good taste

French industry, though not as profitable or as strong as Britain's, was also a source of wealth. Factories (like the one shown in Source 26) produced high-quality goods, especially silk and cotton textiles, wallpapers, furniture and porcelain (see Source 27). All these went to furnish the homes of the bourgeoisie and nobles. Styles of design and painting popular in France at this time became famous for their elegance and 'good taste' in other countries too.

Trade was one way of moving up the social scale. Rich merchants bought country estates in order to acquire a noble's legal privileges.

Financial crisis

In spite of this flourishing trade, the French royal government had no money. Source 28 shows Louis XVI and Jacques Necker, his chief finance minister, gazing in dismay at empty 'treasure chests'. What had gone wrong? Why, when so many people in the country were obviously prosperous, was the government almost bankrupt?

War

There were two main reasons for this economic crisis. The short-term reason was war. As we saw on page 13, France supported the rebels against Britain during the American Revolution of 1775 to 1783. The government had to borrow vast sums of money to pay for the war, and was left with enormous debts. By 1786, the government deficit – the gap between its income and its expenditure – was three times as big as in 1776.

SOURCE 25
French overseas trade in the 18th century.

- Major western European trading port
- → Exports to other parts of Europe
- → Exports to France
- France

SOURCE 26
Women workers in a cloth factory.

LAND AND PEOPLE

SOURCE 27
Elegant French porcelain like this cup and saucer made at Sèvres around 1760, was prized throughout Europe. They are decorated with pure gold.

SOURCE 28
Cartoon showing King Louis XVI (right) and Necker (left) drawn by the British artist, George Cruickshank, in 1788.

1 The French economy was based on producing high-priced luxury goods for the rich. What were the economic dangers in this?

2 Why was it so difficult for the King and his ministers to change the unfair system of taxes?

Taxation

The long-term reason for the government's lack of money was its inefficient system of taxation. The task of collecting taxes was 'sold' to officials, known as 'tax-farmers'. These people were paid out of the taxes they collected, and they often kept some back for themselves. This meant that only part of the money paid as taxes ever reached the royal treasury; the rest was 'lost' along the way.

The taxation system was also unfair. Taxes were demanded from poor peasants, but not from the nobles or bourgeoisie. These two groups claimed to be exempt (free) from taxes, because of ancient privileges.

As a result, the King and his ministers faced the hopeless task of trying to raise taxes from people who had no money (see Source 29), while the wealthiest sections of society, who paid nothing, criticised them for bad management. As Calonne, chief finance minister from 1783 to 1787, declared, it was time the system changed (see Source 30).

'Workmen today need twice as much money to keep them alive, yet they earn no more than fifty years ago'.

SOURCE 29
Comment by parish priest in Normandy, northern France, in the 1780s.

> It is impossible to tax further, ruinous to keep on borrowing, and not enough to confine ourselves to economical reforms ... the only means of managing finally to put the finances truly in order, must consist in revitalising the entire state by re-moulding all that is evil in its workings.

SOURCE 30
Remark by Charles-Alexandre de Calonne, Louis XVI's chief finance minister, in 1787.

LAND AND PEOPLE

Government in crisis

For many years, there had been tensions when *parlements* – especially in Paris – refused to accept new royal laws. The *parlements* had a right to do this if they disagreed with royal policies. To King Louis, it seemed as if *parlements* acted to protect their own interests, not for the good of society. In particular, they blocked attempts at reforming the system by which taxes were collected.

In 1787, Louis and his ministers summoned an assembly of *Notables* (important people) to help them solve France's economic crisis. The *Notables* met and discussed, but would not agree to the government's plans for tax reforms. Meanwhile, the economic problems grew worse. There were demonstrations in provincial cities, supporting local *parlements* against the King. In Paris, starving citizens accused the government of a 'famine plot' – a plan to starve them into obedience – and rioted. In desperation, royal ministers agreed to the *parlements*' calls for a meeting of the Estates-General – the ancient ruling council of France.

SOURCE 32
The meeting of the Estates-General, 5 May 1789.

Voting rights

Before this meeting could take place, there were more disagreements. Who should attend the Estates-General? Traditionally, it was made up of DEPUTIES (elected representatives) from three different groups: First Estate (clergy), Second Estate (nobles), and Third Estate (everyone else). The last time it met, in 1614, there had been an equal number of deputies for each group. Each estate had also voted separately.

- town-dwellers want the same rights and privileges as nobles.
- peasants want freedom from feudal taxes.
- peasants want fewer and fairer royal taxes.
- tithes should be used to support the ordinary parish clergy who helped villagers, and not paid to noble clergy who used it to support their extravagant lifestyle.
- the countryside should not be exploited to make town-dwellers – including nobles – richer.

SOURCE 31
Demands made in the CAHIERS (notebooks listing grievances) drawn up by the ordinary Frenchmen who elected the deputies to represent the Third Estate at the 1789 Estates-General.

LAND AND PEOPLE

SOURCE 33
The historic meeting at the indoor tennis court, June 1789, attended by a few nobles, a few members of the clergy and the Third Estate.

'Go and tell those who have sent you that we sit here by the will of the people, and that we shall not leave except by force of bayonets.'

SOURCE 34
Spoken by the Comte de Mirabeau, on behalf of the Third Estate, while they were meeting at the indoor tennis court, in 1789.

Demands of the Third Estate

The Third Estate now demanded double the number of deputies because they claimed that their members were playing a larger part in French life. They also wanted all sections of the Estates-General to meet at the same time. In this way, the Third Estate would be able to out-vote the other two, who they expected to side with the King.

Third Estate deputies were not poor or disadvantaged like the majority of French people. They were lawyers, officials and rich bourgeois. But, encouraged by other politicians, they felt they were the true 'voice of the nation'. They knew that ordinary people had many grievances which needed to be put right (See Source 31).

'Thus it was that in France the judiciary, the clergy, the rich, gave their original impulse to the Revolution. The people appeared on the scene only later.'

SOURCE 35
Comment by the revolutionary leader, Robespierre, looking back at what happened in 1789.

The start of a Revolution?

The Third Estate's demands had still not been satisfied when the Estates-General held its first meeting in May 1789 (see Source 32). It seemed unlikely that the King and his ministers would give in. The Third Estate was angry and continued to demand that the 'voice of the nation' be heard. On 17 June, they re-named themselves the 'National Assembly'.

Three days later their meeting hall was locked, on government orders. This was, in fact, accidental, but they felt it was a royal attack on their rights and they were furious. They rushed to find another room, and decided to occupy an indoor tennis court (see Source 33). There, they took an oath to stay put until their demands had been met. By 25 June, they had been joined by a majority of deputies from the clergy, plus influential nobles like Mirabeau (see Source 34). On 27 June, the King gave in, and ordered all three Estates to meet together. Was this the start of a Revolution? As Source 35 suggests, the answer is 'yes'.

attainment target

'The French Revolution was begun by good men on good principles' – Tom Paine, writing a few years later.

1. Put this interpretation of the Revolution in your own words.
2. Do you agree with this interpretation? Explain your answer.
3. How far do the sources in these pages support this interpretation?
4. Tom Paine was a supporter of the Revolution. How does that affect your judgement of his interpretation?

UNIT 6

The Revolution

The Revolution begins

On 20 June, 1789, the date of the Tennis Court Oath, the situation was tense, but not dangerous. The king, his officials and his army were still in control of France. At Versailles, nobles, priests and deputies from the Third Estate attending the meeting of the Estates-General, were protesting against the king, but they were not at war with him.

Yet within weeks, angry mobs in Paris could be heard chanting songs like the one in Source 1 and there were riots, murders and massacres (see Source 2). In the countryside, peasants drew up *cahiers*, or lists of complaints against the government, and attacked nobles' property. The French Revolution had begun.

AIMS

In this unit we will look at the events of the French Revolution, during the years 1789 to 1799. We will consider why the Revolution began when it did, and what it hoped to achieve. We will look at the personalities involved, from the royal family to the rebel leaders. Finally, we will see how people reacted to the Revolution, both in France and overseas.

> 'It will be, it will be, it will be
> We'll hang noblemen from the street-lights . . .
> Freedom will be ours for ever
> We'll put an end to cruel tyrants . . .'

SOURCE 1
Popular song, heard on the streets of Paris, 1789.

Events of the Revolution

1789 (14 July)
Bastille attacked; the Revolution begins.

1789 (July–August)
Grand Peur in the countryside – attacks on nobles' property.

1789 (August)
Declaration of the Rights of Man and the Citizen.

1789 (October)
Mob marches to Versailles and captures royal family.

1789 (November)
State take-over of Church property; National Assembly now runs France.

1791 (June)
Royal family tries to escape.

1792 (August)
Fear of invasion after France declares war on Austria; massacres in Paris.

1792 (September)
French troops defeat invaders at Valmy; France attacks nearby lands.

1792 (September)
Monarchy abolished.

1792 (December)
Louis XVI on trial.

1793 (January)
Louis XVI executed.

1793 (March)
France now at war with most other European powers.

1793 (March)
Vendée revolt by anti-revolutionaries.

1793 (April)
Committee of Public Safety (radicals) now controls government.

1793 (May)
Anti-revolutionary revolts in Lyon and Bordeaux. Disputes among revolutionary leaders.

1793 (June)
Girondin (moderate) leaders arrested; reign of Terror begins.

1793 (July)
Marat assassinated; Jacobin (radical) leader Robespierre seizes power.

1793 (August)
Conscription introduced.

1793 (October)
Marie Antoinette executed, also many Girondins (moderates).

1794 (October)
New revolutionary religion introduced.

1794 (April)
Danton (radical) executed.

1794 (July)
Robespierre executed; Terror ends.

1795 (November)
Directory (moderates) now rules France; wars continue in Europe.

1799 (November)
Napoleon seizes power.

THE REVOLUTION

SOURCE 2
The march to Versailles, October 1789. Officers of the Royal Guard who resisted the revolutionaries were beheaded and their heads carried on spikes.

Reasons for the Revolution
Why did the Revolution break out in 1789? There were many different reasons. Some were long term, others were more immediate.

In the countryside:
People were discontented, because of:
- poverty among the peasants
- wide gap between rich and poor
- heavy taxes
- privileges of the nobles

New developments in the 18th century:
- growing wealth of the bourgeoisie
- low wages for town workers
- new scientific and philosophical ideas
- the Revolution in America

Personalities:
- Louis XVI was lazy and incompetent
- Marie Antoinette was extravagant
- their son was dying, so they neglected politics
- people did not trust royal ministers
- new leaders emerged in the Estates-General

Events, 1787 to 1789:
- the government ran short of money
- calling the Estates-General made people hope for change
- harvests were bad and people were hungry

What were the aims of the Revolution?
There is no simple answer. Protesters wanted to get rid of a system which they felt was unfair. They hoped the Estates-General would find a solution. As Sources 3, 4, 5 and 6 reveal, people reacted to the Revolution in different ways.

'I believe that some extraordinary event is likely to occur'.

SOURCE 3
Comment by Antoine-Joseph Barnarve (1761–1793), a lawyer who supported the Revolution in its early days.

'Bliss was it in that dawn to be alive. And to be young, was very heaven.'

SOURCE 4
From 'The Prelude', a poem by the English poet, William Wordsworth, who visited France in 1789.

> Like everyone else, I was shaking with terror ... waiting for the royalists to come and murder us ... (but) we went about our business as we would on any other day.

SOURCE 5
Revolutionary violence in 1792 remembered by Marie-Victoire Monnard, an apprentice seamstress, aged 13.

'My ambition is that one day I may live, in the country, with a wife and children, with books for my spare time, and, for the rest, time to spare for the poor among my neighbours.'

SOURCE 6
Louis-Antoine de Saint-Just (1767–1794), a young revolutionary, explaining what he hoped for after the Revolution.

THE REVOLUTION

The events of 1789

Today, over 200 years after the French Revolution, 14 July is a national holiday in France. Why is this date so important? It is because, on that day in 1789, a crowd of angry people in Paris rushed to the royal prison called the Bastille, forced their way in and released the prisoners. They murdered the governor and many guards (see Source 7). 'Bastille Day' marks the start of the French Revolution.

There were, in fact, only 14 prisoners inside the Bastille, and none had been imprisoned for political reasons. To the Paris mob however, the Bastille was important as a symbol of royal power. They hated the King and his ministers, and wanted to run the country for themselves.

Mob rule?

Onlookers, like the ROYALIST sympathiser quoted in Source 8, realised that the attack on the Bastille marked a new kind of discontent in France. For the first time, ordinary people were taking part in politics. Representatives from all sections of French society – nobles, clergy, bourgeoisie and ordinary citizens – were united against the King. For a while, it even seemed as if ordinary people were the revolutionary leaders. As well as massacres in Paris, there were murders in the countryside. Documents recording peasants' duty to pay tax, and nobles' ancient privileges, were destroyed by villagers. There were riots in many towns, too. People called this hot, dangerous, summertime the Great Fear (see Source 9).

attainment target

1 List three long-term and three short-term causes of the French Revolution. Explain how you have decided which are long- and which are short-term.

2 Choose one example of each and explain how it led to revolution.

3 Describe how money and finance link several of the causes listed on page 77.

4 Which of the causes listed do you think was the most important? Explain your answer.

SOURCE 7
The attack on the Bastille, 14 July 1789. A painting made soon after the event, by Dubois.

'The aristocracy is at an end, the clergy wobbles on the edge of mindlessness, and the Third Estate doesn't really understand what is going on. Only the victorious mob is happy, with nothing to lose, all to gain.'

SOURCE 8
Comment by Count Axel von Fersen, a close friend of the royal family, 1789.

SOURCE 9
An attack on a noble's castle during the Great Fear in the summer of 1789.

THE REVOLUTION

SOURCE 10
Parisian women march to Versailles, October 1789.

We want bread!

In Paris, rioting continued throughout the autumn. It came to a climax on 5 and 6 October, when thousands of women, exasperated at not being able to buy food for their families, marched to the royal palace at Versailles (see Source 10). They surrounded the King, and forced him and his family to come back to Paris with them. Even though the royal family lodged in another royal palace, the Tuileries, from now on the King was in their power.

The Rights of Man

Members of the National Assembly disagreed about whether the summer's violence – some of which was directed against their own property – was acceptable. Most thought it was not, but they had to show support for the mob's revolutionary enthusiasm, to protect their homes and businesses from further damage. Of course, many Assembly members also genuinely believed that the time had come to make changes in the way France was run. So, on 4 August, they passed a decree abolishing FEUDALISM, the ancient network of rights, privileges and taxes which the peasants hated so much. They followed this, on 26 August, by the solemn 'Declaration of the Rights of Man and the Citizen' (Source 11). This set out clearly what the Assembly hoped the Revolution would achieve. You can read more about it on page 80.

SOURCE 11
A revolutionary painting recording the Declaration of the Rights of Man and the Citizen.

THE REVOLUTION

Revolutionary reforms

Late in 1789, two new questions concerned the National Assembly. How could they stop the Revolution leading to complete ANARCHY (lack of government), and what new laws should they make to replace the old ones? Forceful speakers appeared, arguing for dozens of different policies. As one of the Assembly's leaders, Mirabeau, (pictured in Source 12), complained, it was not always easy to keep eager revolutionaries under control (Source 13).

Freedom and equality

As we saw on page 79, the National Assembly had approved a 'Declaration of the Rights of Man and the Citizen'. It stated bravely that:

- Men are born and remain free.
- They have equal rights to liberty, property, security and freedom from tyranny.
- Laws should reflect citizens' wishes.
- All citizens should be able to make their political views known.
- Liberty is the freedom to do anything that doesn't harm anybody else.
- Everyone should have the right of free speech.

SOURCE 12
The Comte de Mirabeau (1749–1791), painted in 1790.

'When you agree to take charge of a revolution, the difficulty is not making it move, but controlling it.'

SOURCE 13
Comment by Mirabeau, looking back on the events of the Revolution shortly before his death in 1791.

SOURCE 14
The Cordeliers Church, in Paris, being destroyed following the State take-over of Church property.

Active citizens

How could this Declaration be put into practice? Partly by giving the Assembly more power. In 1789, the deputies changed Louis XVI's title from 'King of France' to 'King of the French'. Now the land no longer belonged to him. In 1791, they passed laws to allow more people to take part in politics. The richest men (65 per cent of them) were called 'active citizens'. They could vote, and choose judges, bishops, tax collectors and members of the Assembly. Poorer people and women could not vote.

The legal and local government systems were also reformed. Inherited noble titles were abolished; everyone was now equal in the eyes of the law. Trial by jury was introduced, and torture was banned. Instead of the old regions, ruled over by PARLEMENTS, 83 new DÉPARTEMENTS were created, controlled by central government.

ACTIVITY

Work in a small group to discuss these questions:
1. If you were drawing up a list of new laws to improve 18th century French society, what would be the three most important reforms?
2. Do you think the people who drew up the Declaration of the Rights of Man and the Citizen did a good job?
3. What three new laws would you like to introduce to improve our society today?

THE REVOLUTION

A national Church?

In November 1789, the Assembly decided to 'nationalise' the church. It distrusted priests' vows of obedience to the Pope in Rome, and disliked the Church's support for the King. Church lands and buildings were taken over and destroyed (see Source 14) or sold off, using ASSIGNATS (paper money). You can see these in Source 15. Monasteries and nunneries were closed down, and priests were asked to swear loyalty to the state. Many refused.

Celebrations

Not everyone in France benefited from these changes, and not everyone agreed with them, but it was becoming dangerous to speak out. Defiant priests and old-style royalists were put in prison. Most French people, especially those in Paris, probably shared the views of the speaker quoted in Source 16. They happily joined in celebrations, like the festival shown in Source 17, to mark the Revolution's first 'anniversary' on 14 July 1790.

SOURCE 15
Assignats being exchanged for cash by country people.

'A new political structure is being built. I do not say it is absolutely perfect, but it is sufficient to guarantee liberty.'

SOURCE 16
Remark by the Marquis de Lafayette (1757–1834), a nobleman who sympathised with the Revolution.

SOURCE 17
Celebrations known as 'The Festival of the Federation', held in Paris on 14 July 1790.

THE REVOLUTION

SOURCE 18
Popular woodcut showing the royal family making their bid to escape from France, 1791.

Kill the king

For over a year, the King and his family lived like prisoners in Paris. Observers reported that Louis seemed depressed and Marie Antoinette looked old and ill. Many of their friends fled abroad for safety. The King and Queen sent secret letters to them, and to royalists in France. They also asked foreign rulers for help, especially Marie Antoinette's family in Austria.

> 'If this country ceases to be a monarchy it will be entirely the fault of Louis XVI. Blunder upon blunder ... have been the destruction of his reign.'
> *Lord Gower, a British aristocrat*
>
> 'The absence of a king is more desirable than his presence ... He has abdicated (given up) his throne by having fled from his post.'
> *Tom Paine, a British campaigner for freedom*
>
> 'We will eat her heart and liver.'
> *A mob of French citizens*

SOURCE 19
Comments by people from different levels of society with different views about the King and Queen.

Escape to Varennes

On 20 June 1791, the royal family decided to try to escape. At night, (with Louis disguised as a servant) they left Paris in a horse-drawn coach (Source 18). They headed towards Luxembourg, where the Emperor of Austria had 8,000 troops. There were also loyal French soldiers nearby. But the King was stopped at Varennes, a village not far from the border. The local postmaster recognised him from his portrait on a 50-*livre* (pound) note. Louis refused to run away, because that would mean leaving his wife and children behind. The royal family were sent back to Paris under armed guard. Hostile crowds shouted insults all along the way.

'Louis the False'

What did Louis think about the Revolution? In public, he claimed to support the various revolutionary governments, and to accept their new laws. However he left a note behind him when he tried to escape, protesting that he felt injured and powerless, and that the Revolution was ruining France. After that, very few people trusted him. He became known as 'Louis the False'. Source 19 gives three comments made about Louis and Marie Antoinette after their bid to escape.

The end of royal power

In August 1792, crowds attacked the Tuileries (Source 20). Over 700 soldiers were hacked to death, and the King and Queen were threatened. It was a terrifying moment. From now on, the King and all royalists were treated like traitors. They were put in prison, and the King was deprived of all his powers.

THE REVOLUTION

The following month (September), Prussian and Austrian troops marched towards Paris, hoping to free the King. Frightened of what might happen if they reached the city, panic-stricken crowds attacked the prisons and killed the royalists there.

Once again, Louis' life was spared by the mob. But for how long? On 21 September, in the new Assembly (now called the Convention), members voted to abolish the monarchy, and set up a republic. The King was no longer part of government. To many people, he seemed a dangerous, useless burden to France.

Innocent or guilty?

In December 1792, King Louis was put on trial. The Convention accused him of over 30 'crimes against the state'. Sources 21 and 22 record what two leading deputies from the Convention said in court. All 693 deputies found Louis guilty, and the majority (374) voted for his death. He was executed by guillotine (Source 23) on 21 January 1793. On the scaffold, he said, 'I die innocent'.

> **attainment target**
>
> Look at the following reasons for Louis' execution:
>
> a) His policy as King up to 1789;   b) his attitude to the Revolution;   c) the flight to Varennes;   d) foreign troops invading France;   e) the declaration of a republic.
>
> 1 Choose two of these reasons and say how they helped bring about Louis' execution.
>
> 2 Which of the reasons above were his fault and which were not?
>
> 3 Which do you think was the most important reason? Compare your choice with those you rejected.

'Monarchy is not a crime – it is THE crime.'

SOURCE 22
Comment by Louis-Antoine Saint-Just (1767–1794), a young revolutionary leader.

SOURCE 23
Souvenir plate showing the execution of Louis XVI.

SOURCE 20
Parisian citizens attack the royal palace of the Tuileries, 10 August 1792.

'You should fill tyrants with terror – I vote for the penalty of death..'

SOURCE 21
Spoken by Georges-Jacques Danton (1759–1794), one of the revolutionary leaders, at Louis XVI's trial.

MAKING CONNECTIONS

Was revolution inevitable?

As we have seen, England was in turmoil in 1642. By 1789, events in France had also led to a crisis. To many people, England in 1642 and France in 1789 seemed balanced on the edge of revolution. But were things really the same in both countries? Was the history of England merely repeating itself in France? King Charles I of England and King Louis XVI of France both lost their heads, but how similar – or different – were the causes of those dramatic, bloody executions?

Bound to happen?

Some historians have also suggested that, in England in 1642 and in France in 1789, revolutions were 'bound to happen'. They argue that the kings and their ministers were inevitably going to be overthrown. They could no longer rule because they had no money, people no longer trusted them, and they had lost the support of Parliament (in England) or the Estates-General (in France). These assemblies were made up of the most powerful people in the country: landowners, churchmen, scholars, lawyers and other professionals. Without their co-operation, weak kings could not run local government, collect taxes, try court cases or control the 'mob' of poor ordinary people, who might rise in rebellion if economic conditions grew too bad. Do you think that these pre-conditions for an 'inevitable revolution' existed both in England and in France?

ACTIVITY

The historical 'turning points' of 1642 and 1789 are separated from one another by about 150 years (to say nothing of big differences in language, culture and religion). Yet historians have often drawn parallels between them. Here are some key questions to help us compare conditions in England in 1642 and France in 1789.

1. Who was protesting against royal government?
2. What were their main complaints?
3. Were these complaints about long-term grievances or short-term problems, or both?
4. Did the protesters just want to change the existing system or to make radical changes to it?
5. How did kings react to these complaints?
6. How did the personalities of the kings and their families affect events?

Copy out the chart below and write your answers to these six key questions in the first and second columns of the chart. You can find information to help you answer these questions by studying pages 40 to 45 and 70 to 77 of this book, and by looking at Sources 24 to 33 opposite. When you have done this, compare the situation in England in 1642 with France in 1789 and record your conclusions by putting ticks in either the third column or the fourth column of the chart.

Question Number	England 1642	France 1789	Similar?	Different?
1				
2				
3				
4				
5				
6				

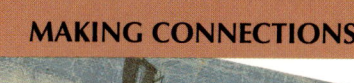

MAKING CONNECTIONS

SOURCE 24
The execution of Charles I, 1649.

SOURCE 25
The execution of Louis XVI, 1793.

Old loyalties?

'My only concern now is to follow my master. I have served him for 30 years and will not do so base a thing as to desert him now.'

SOURCE 26
Written in 1642 by Sir Edmund Verney, a country gentleman who reluctantly supported Charles I.

'I would like my country to be as free [as America] providing it would not destroy our monarchy, our status and our traditions.'

SOURCE 27
Written by a French nobleman.

Complaints

 No taxes unless agreed by Parliament.

SOURCE 28
Demand by MPs, 1640.

'All the peasants here are getting ready to refuse the tithe [tax] collectors . . .'

SOURCE 29
From a list of complaints by peasants in Brittany, 1789.

Beliefs and wishes

 It is the Lord's cause we stand for.

SOURCE 30
Letter from Lady Brilliana Harley (who supported the Parliamentarians) 1642.

'You can never rule a people against its wishes.'

SOURCE 31
Letter from Louis XVI, 1791.

Who should rule?

'All affairs of state, including foreign policy, religion and finance, must be agreed with Parliament.'

SOURCE 32
From the 'Nineteen Propositions' – demands made by Parliament, 1642.

All the power of the nation rests with the common people – the state exists for them, and them alone.

SOURCE 33
Comment by anti-royalist French nobleman, 1788.

THE REVOLUTION

Reactions at home

The execution of the King in January 1793 changed France for ever. Some people thought this was a good thing; some did not. For royalists, it marked the end of 'the good old days' and the beginning of a nightmare period of uncertainty and chaos. For revolutionaries, it was the start of a bright new future for republican France.

Even among those who sympathised with the Revolution, there were disagreements. Deputies elected to the National Convention (the new government which replaced the revolutionaries' National Assembly and the Confederation which developed from it) – were mostly MODERATES. They supported firm law and order, and wanted to protect private property. More and more, they found themselves quarrelling with leaders of the ordinary people of Paris – the SANS-CULOTTES.

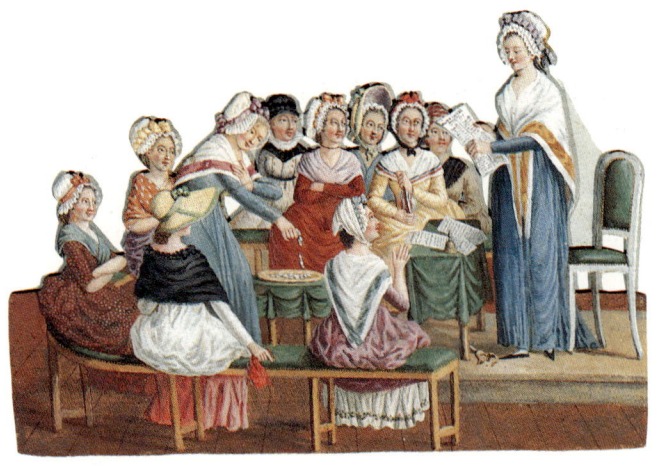

SOURCE 35
A meeting of the Patriotic (revolutionary) Women's Club in Paris.

'The moment has arrived for women to throw away their shameful laziness . . . Ignorance, pride and men's power have kept them quiet for too long. Let us return to the past when our proud fore-mothers spoke at public meetings and fought with weapons alongside the men.'

SOURCE 36
Part of a speech by Théroigne de Méricourt, one of the leading women revolutionaries.

Equality

'*Sans-culottes*' meant 'no breeches', or 'wearing rough, working clothes' (see Source 34). Noblemen often wore waistcoats and knee-breeches made of embroidered satin, while *sans-culottes* wore plain shirts, long baggy trousers and woollen jackets. They often chose the revolutionary colours of red, white and blue. Even *sans-culottes* who could afford better clothes preferred this 'uniform'; it was a way of showing that they believed all men were equal.

Disagreements

Sans-culottes clashed with the deputies over three main issues. They wanted all adult men to be given the right to vote. They demanded regular food supplies and low prices. Most RADICAL of all, they wanted the amount of land, money or property that anyone could own to be limited by law, so that wealth could be shared out equally.

SOURCE 34
A popular Parisian singer, Chenard, who supported the *sans-culottes*, in typical *sans-culotte* clothes.

Revolutionary women

Ordinary women played an important part in revolutionary events but, on the whole, their contribution was ignored by the (male) deputies, and by the (male) leaders of the *sans-culottes*. The 'Declaration of the Rights of Man and the Citizen' did not include women in its reforms. In the early years of the Revolution, women's groups (like the one in Source 35) met to discuss politics. Some carried weapons, but they were quickly banned. This did not stop leaders like Théroigne de Méricourt (quoted in Source 36) urging women to fight for their beliefs alongside revolutionary men.

Provincial rebels

There had always been differences of opinion between go-ahead Paris, and the slower, more cautious, country districts of France. Now, in 1793, these quarrels turned into a bloody war. Many people living in the PROVINCES felt that the Parisian *sans-culottes* were too radical. They thought that the nationalisation of the Church and the execution of the King had been wrong. Source 37 shows the areas where these views had most support. Thousands of men and women were killed (see Source 38). Source 39 shows fighting close to the city of Lyon, where peasants and town-dwellers attacked revolutionary leaders and other republicans.

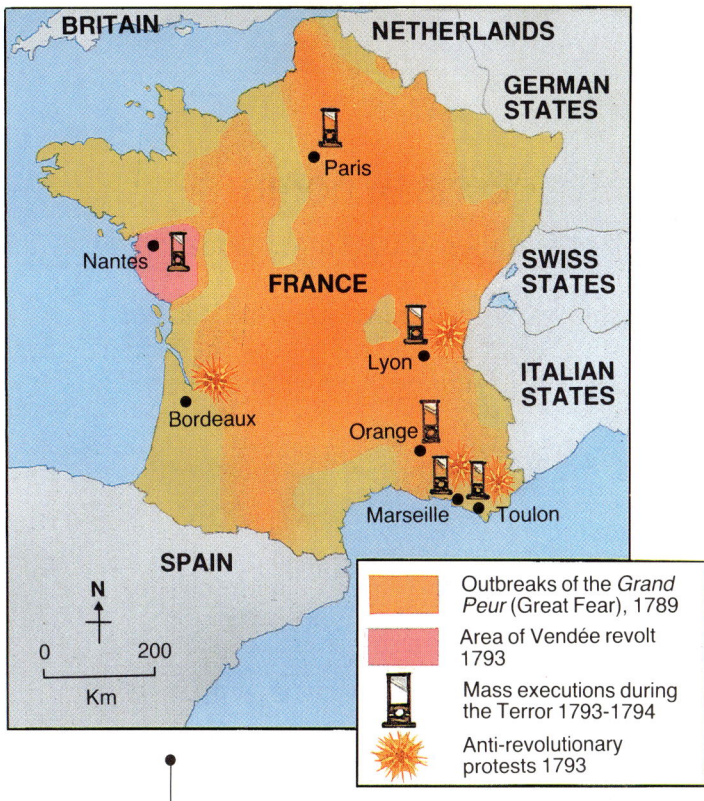

SOURCE 37
Royalist and revolutionary areas of France.

'Every wickedness you can imagine. About 50 people were beaten and their heads shaved. It seems that the women were most unpopular with the attackers. Three died a little later. The remainder are still weak.'

SOURCE 38
Description of fighting between revolutionaries and royalists near Rouen, in northern France, 1792.

1. Read about the demands made by the *sans-culottes* on page 86. How can you tell from these that the *sans-culottes* were city-based?
2. Why do you think there was more support for the Revolution in the city of Paris than in the countryside?
3. Why are clothes so often a sign of rebellion? Give some present day examples of this.

SOURCE 39
Fighting between revolutionaries and royalists in the important city of Lyon, in southern France, 1795.

THE REVOLUTION

Reactions abroad

On page 83 we saw that, in 1792, Parisian citizens had been frightened when enemy troops began to advance, so they killed royalist prisoners. In fact, the citizens' fears were unnecessary. The threatened invasion never came. Revolutionary troops attacked the enemy armies at Valmy, on the road to Paris, and they retreated in confusion. The invaders had not expected these 'rebel' soldiers to be so strong.

Exporting the Revolution

This surprising victory gave great encouragement to the revolutionary leaders. It made them think it might be possible for France to 'export' its revolutionary ideas. Source 40 tell us what two revolutionaries hoped to achieve. By the end of 1792, French soldiers were advancing into Belgium, Germany and Savoy, as you can see from Source 41.

France's revolutionary ambitions horrified most governments in Europe. In 1793, England, Spain and the Netherlands joined Austria and Prussia, which were already enemies of France. Austria, led by its confident new Emperor Francis II (see Source 42), was especially eager to attack. Austrians were outraged when Marie Antoinette was guillotined in October 1793.

In 1794, France conquered the Netherlands, and set up a revolutionary government there. A stirring new song, called 'La Marseillaise', was composed for these revolutionary soldiers to sing. In 1795, it was adopted as the French national anthem, and it remains so today. You can see the words and music in Source 43.

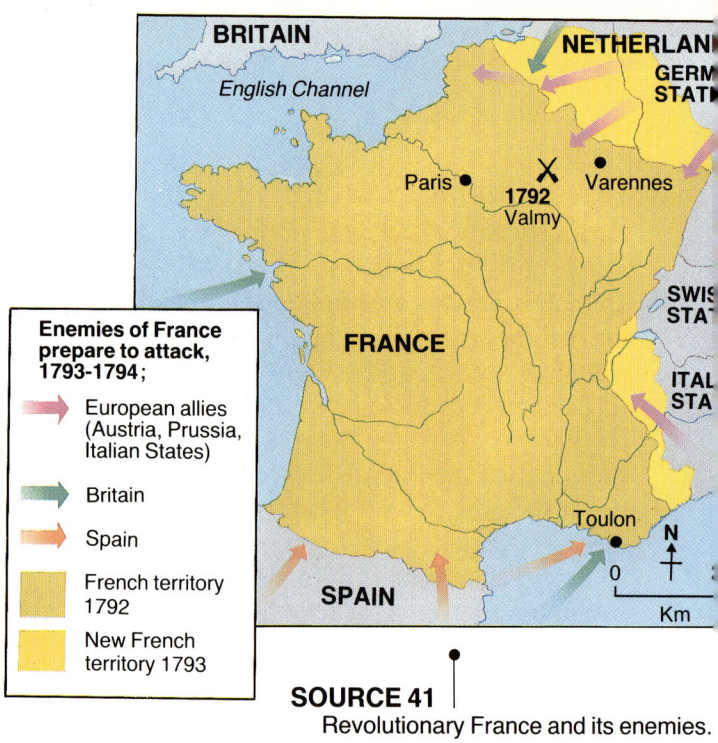

SOURCE 41
Revolutionary France and its enemies.

SOURCE 42
Emperor Francis II of Austria (1768–1835), a determined opponent of revolutionary France.

Renewing the state

Revolutionary leaders in France thought that war should be encouraged for another reason, too – it was good for people at home. It allowed them to forget their quarrels with one another while they were united against a foreign enemy. As Source 44 reveals, it could also be used by the government to send critics of the Revolution out of the country.

A war of ideas

European nations did not fight France only on the battlefield. They took part in a war of ideas. The Irishman, Edmund Burke, wrote 'Reflections on the Revolution in France' (1790), which fiercely criticised revolutionary leaders. British artists portrayed the French as bloodthirsty monsters in cartoons such as Source 45.

> 'We must never rest until all Europe is in flames ... We must inflame every mind either to rebel or to accept revolution.'

> 'We can be reborn only through bloodshed.'

SOURCE 40
Comments by (above) the revolutionary journalist Jacques-Pierre Brissot (1754–1793) and (below) the revolutionary political hostess Manon Roland (1754–1793).

THE REVOLUTION

SOURCE 43
Song-sheet showing the French Army of the Rhine, marching to fight in Germany, plus words and music of the Marseillaise.

SOURCE 45
Cartoon by the English artist, James Gillray, after Louis XVI's bid to escape from France. Gillray has drawn the members of the National Assembly as monsters, gleefully discussing what to do with the King.

> France ... needs war to consolidate its freedom. It needs war to get rid of the wickedness of tyranny. It needs war to drive out those who might poison liberty.

SOURCE 44
Another piece of revolutionary propaganda written by Brissot (see Source 40).

Ending slavery

There were few slaves in France itself, but the economy of most French colonies, particularly in the Caribbean, depended on slave labour. During the Revolution, many politicians argued that it was wrong to fight for equality at home, while ignoring the lack of freedom in French lands overseas. In 1788, they had founded 'Friends of Black Peoples', a campaigning group which aimed to abolish slavery. Slaves in the French colony of San Domingo (Haiti) rebelled in 1794, encouraged by revolutionary events in France. Their courageous leader, Toussaint L'Ouverture, is pictured in Source 46.

SOURCE 46
Toussaint L'Ouverture (left, front of picture) and his troops in Haiti.

THE REVOLUTION

Revolutionary leaders

All revolutions need someone to lead them, to make new policies and to decide what action is required to carry them out. We have seen how, in the early days of the Revolution, two very different groups were active: deputies of the National Assembly (and the later assemblies that followed it) and the Paris mob, known as the *sans-culottes*.

Individual revolutionaries

Individuals also acted as leaders, like the churchman, Canon Sieyès of Chartres, who drafted important schemes for reform. More practical leaders included two nobles: the Marquis de Lafayette and the Comte de Mirabeau. Lafayette had fought for the rebels during the American Revolution. He commanded the French army until 1792, when he left France, shocked by the King's execution. Mirabeau (page 80) was a rousing speaker, who played a leading part in the events of summer 1789. However he thought the *sans-culottes* were too extreme, and secretly supported the King. If he had not died in 1791, he would probably have been executed as a traitor.

There were other revolutionary leaders who were not nobles. They met in cafés and SALONS of Paris to discuss their ideas. *Salons* were rooms in private houses, where people who shared similar ideas met. Privacy was needed because rival groups soon began to hold different views.

Girondins and Jacobins

The two most important FACTIONS were the GIRONDINS and the JACOBINS. At first, they had been allies. However, moderate Girondins, like Brissot (Source 47), and Madame Roland (see Source 48) criticised Jacobins' radical ideas. Later, many Girondins were executed by the Jacobins, led by Danton (Source 49) and Robespierre (Source 50).

SOURCE 47
Jacques-Pierre Brissot (1754–1793). Journalist and campaigner. Founder of anti-slavery society: Friends of Black People (see page 89). Member of Legislative Assembly; thought Paris mob was too violent. Executed by Jacobins October 1793.

'At fourteen, as now, I was about five feet tall, having reached full growth. I had trim legs, very well-shaped feet . . . straight shoulders, a steady and graceful posture, and brisk, light footsteps. My face was not really remarkable, save for its genuine freshness and much sweetness. My mouth is rather large; you could notice a thousand people who are prettier but no child with a more tender and seductive smile . . . My complexion is striking . . . my skin soft, my arms rounded, my hands not small, but attractive with long slender fingers suggesting cleverness combined with grace . . .'

SOURCE 48
Manon Roland (1754–1793). From a Paris craft-worker's family. Clever and ambitious. Held a salon where the Girondins met. With her husband, very active in politics. Arrested by Jacobins and executed November 1793.

attainment target

1. What do Sources 51 and 52 tell us about Charlotte Corday?
2. Which of Sources 52 and 53 is more valuable for finding out about her motives?
3. What does Source 53 tell us about the Tribunal's view of women?
4. Write an account of the murder of Marat using these sources.

THE REVOLUTION

SOURCE 50
Maximilien Robespierre (1758–1794). Educated as a lawyer. Member of Legislative Assembly and a Jacobin. Called 'the incorruptible', because he did not make money out of his position. Wanted to exterminate 'enemies of the Revolution' (see page 92). Executed by new, moderate leaders appalled by his violence, July 1794.

SOURCE 49
Georges Danton (1759–1794). Educated as a lawyer. Rich, popular, very powerful politician. Originally supported the Jacobins, but disagreed with their policy of mass execution (see page 92). Executed on Robespierre's orders April 1794.

The Murder of Marat

One of the best-known events of the Revolution happened in 1793, when the Girondin supporter, Charlotte Corday, killed Jean-Paul Marat, a popular Jacobin, in his bath. Source 51 reports Corday's words explaining why she committed the murder. Source 52 shows the murder scene. Source 53 comes from the revolutionary Tribunal (court) proceedings, organised by the Jacobins. Corday was tried by this court, and executed the same day.

'Oh my native land – your misfortunes are breaking my heart; all I can sacrifice to you is my life.'

SOURCE 51
From a note found pinned to Charlotte Corday's clothes, after her execution.

SOURCE 52
A contemporary painting of the murder of Marat by Charlotte Corday.

Jean-Paul Marat (1744–1793) Doctor, admired by Parisians. Member of the Assembly. Ran newspaper 'The People's Friend', criticising Girondins and all rich people. Feared by some for his violent policies.

Charlotte Corday (1768–1793) Educated woman, active in politics in Normandy. Supported Girondins. Believed that Marat's policies would lead to terrible bloodshed, so killed him. Hated by Jacobins. Executed July 1793.

'She was a woman who gave up womanliness . . . romantic love and other tendernesses no longer affect a woman who seeks knowledge, wit, scholarship, philosophy, and who hopes for personal fame. Decent men dislike such females . . .'

SOURCE 53
From the record kept by the Revolutionary Tribunal, 1793.

SOURCE 54
Cartoon criticising the Terror. The pyramid-shaped tombstone reads 'Here lies all of France'.

SOURCE 55
A meeting of a revolutionary TRIBUNAL (court) held on 2–3 September, 1792.

The Terror

From March 1793 to August 1794, between 14,000 and 17,000 French men and women were executed. A further 24,000 died in prison, or were killed by revolutionary armies. A 'modern' French machine, the guillotine (Source 54), was used for executions. It was invented as a kinder way of killing people than the axe, but it soon became feared as a symbol of revolutionary power. Looking back, people called the years 1793–1794 'the Terror'. Why did this bloodshed take place?

Defending the Revolution

In 1793, leaders of the Revolution felt under threat. They faced rebellion from royalists at home and invasion from enemies abroad. To cope with these dangers, a Committee of Public Safety was appointed. Its most important members were Jacobins: Danton and Robespierre. Committee members felt it was their duty to defend the Revolution, at all costs. In this emergency situation, the safest thing would be to rid France of anyone who dared criticise revolutionary ideas.

In June 1793, Girondin members of the Convention were expelled, and a new constitution was introduced. In September 1793, the Committee passed a law saying that all people suspected of anti-revolutionary views should be put in prison. If found guilty, they should be killed. You can see suspects being interrogated in Source 55. Neighbourhood 'thought police' were appointed, and conscription – forced enrolment – to the 'Peoples' Army' was introduced.

'The only way to establish a Republic is to utterly destroy all opposition.'

'I recognise as a patriot only that man who will, if necessary, betray his father, mother and sister, and then drink a glass of their blood on the scaffold.'

SOURCE 56
The views of two Jacobins during the Terror.

Who was killed?			
By rank in society:		By region:	
Nobles	900	Paris	2,600
Lawyers/officials	300	Vendée (area of royalist rebellion)	8,700
Bourgeoisie	3,500		
Priests	900		
Ordinary workers	4,500	Royalist cities	2,000
Peasants	4,000	Royalist south	1,300
Others	200	Others	2,000
Total	14,300	Total	16,600
(Exact totals are impossible; it depends which sources are used.)			

THE REVOLUTION

Reactions to the Terror

Reactions to the Terror were mixed. Even its leaders could not agree whether the policy of mass executions was right. But those who dared voice their opposition (like Danton) were sent to the guillotine. Source 56 shows how some Committee members justified their actions; Source 57 reports a horrified comment from a moderate onlooker.

A new France

Not all the policies introduced by the Committee of Public Safety were violent. Some were designed to help ordinary people, for example fixing maximum prices for food and distributing guilty suspects' goods to the poor. A new calendar (Source 58) was established, to mark the beginning of the revolutionary era. In 1794, slavery was abolished.

A new way of speaking to other people, using the familiar form of the word 'you', ('tu') rather than the formal 'vous', was introduced. Like the modern word 'comrade', it was meant to show that, after the Revolution, everyone was equal. Villages and towns changed their names; for example, Roiville (Kingstown) became Peupleville (Peopletown). Patriotic parents named their children after revolutionary heroes, like Voltaire. Others abandoned 'Christian' names and chose names from nature, such as *Blé* (Wheat), *Myrthe* (Myrtle) or *Safran* (Saffron).

> Look at the lists opposite of people killed during the terror.
>
> 1 Which group suffered the most deaths?
> 2 What do these figures tell us about:
>   - the people most affected by the Revolution?
>   - the people most hated or feared by Jacobins?
>   - the differences between Paris and elsewhere?
> 3 Is it true that the Revolution was a rebellion of poor people against a rich ruling class?

 The Revolution . . . is devouring its own children.

SOURCE 57
Comment made by the Frenchman, Pierre-Victurnien Vernigand during the Terror. Compare this with Source 56.

SOURCE 58
The new calendar introduced to mark the beginning of the revolutionary era.

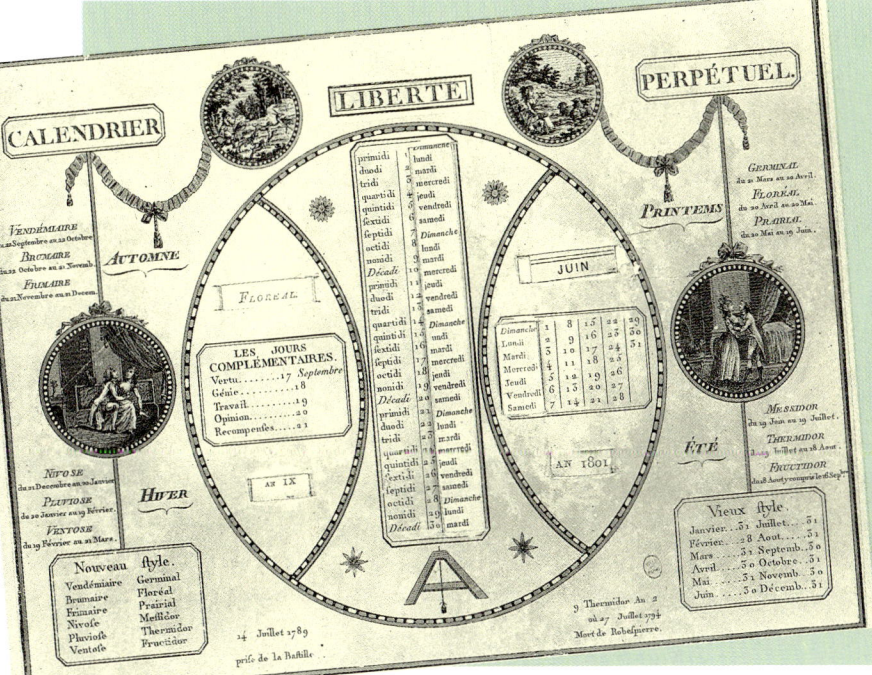

The Revolutionary Calendar

The Convention made a new calendar for France. It had 12 months, but each month was divided into three weeks of 10 days each. The months were as follows:–

Vendémiaire	Grape harvest	22 September–21 October
Brumaire	Misty	22 October–20 November
Frimaire	Frosty	21 November–20 December
Nivôse	Snowy	21 December–19 January
Pluviose	Rainy	20 January–18 February
Ventôse	Windy	19 February–20 March
Germinal	Month of buds	21 March–19 April
Floréal	Flower month	20 April–19 May
Prairial	Meadow month	20 May–18 June
Messidor	Harvest month	19 June–18 July
Thermidor	Month of heat	19 July–17 August
Fructidor	Month of fruits	18 August–16 September

The five days left over at the end of the year were holidays. Each new year started on 22 September (or 1 Vendémiaire), with 1 Vendémiaire 1793 marking the start of the first year of the Republic.

93

THE REVOLUTION

The end of the Revolution

Robespierre and his allies on the Committee of Public Safety were guillotined by moderate politicians in July 1794. The Terror was over. Better still, from the new government's point of view, its terrifying policies were no longer necessary. Moderates had shown they could win control.

Throughout France, the strongest feeling was probably one of relief. Even if most French people did not agree with British onlookers, who called Robespierre a 'butcher', they felt that too many 'enemies of the Revolution' had died. Even today, historians do not all hold the same opinions about Robespierre's career. Was he simply power-mad, or was he boldly trying to force through policies which he really believed would help the ordinary citizens of France?

> 'The rebels' guns are aiming at the city . . . the outskirts are packed with squads of citizens bearing pikes and a few old-style muskets . . . the people seem determined not to be disarmed. Women have gathered in every street, and are making uproar . . .'

SOURCE 59
From Paris police records.

SOURCE 60
Rich, fashionable, anti-revolutionary young men, known as *Incroyables* ('Unbelievables').

SOURCE 61
Troops led by Napoleon Bonaparte defeat citizens rebelling against the government, 5 October 1795.

Reconstruction

The politicians who took over from Robespierre had a difficult task. They had to restore calm and trust in the government and rebuild trade and industry, while supporting the Revolution. They also had to control royalist rebels in the provinces. As Source 59 reveals, fighting was still going on. In Paris, Jacobins were attacked by rich, anti-revolutionary young men (see Source 60), and the Jacobin club was closed down. Officials appointed during the Terror lost their jobs and even the word 'revolutionary' was banned. On 5 October 1795, a group of royalists attempted to seize power (see Source 61). They were defeated, thanks to the quick thinking of a young officer named Napoleon.

The Directory

At the end of 1795, five politicians known as 'the DIRECTORY' took over the government (see Source 62). Their policies were anti-royalist, and they did not want the Terror to return, but they were not popular (see Source 63). They struggled to cope with France's economic crisis. As always, it had to confront many rival groups with different views, all wanting power.

The Directory felt that the Revolution was only likely to survive if France was united against a foreign enemy. It therefore encouraged wars against other European states. However, in spite of victories, such as Napoleon's success at the battle of Rivoli in 1796 (pictured in Source 64), the new government still did not win peoples' support. By 1799, secret groups of conspirators were seeking change.

SOURCE 62
The first public meeting of the Directory, November 1795. A 19th century engraving.

Royalist or republican?

One group, the royalists, thought it would be a good idea to invite Louis XVI's brother to head a new national government, though with strictly limited powers. The other group, the republicans, hated the idea of a return to royal rule. They wanted to run the government themselves. So they asked Napoleon – by now, France's most famous soldier – to back them. With the army on their side, they believed they could govern France. But events did not turn out as they had planned.

1 Why did the Terror happen?
2 Why did it stop after the death of Robespierre?
3 Why do you think the new government banned the word 'revolutionary?'
4 Do you think that the Directory's policy of war against foreigners was likely to work?

'A better 'organised' constitution has never yet been organised by human wisdom.'

SOURCE 63
Sarcastic comment about the Directory by the revolutionary politician, Tom Paine.

SOURCE 64
The battle of Rivoli, 1797, painted by Felix Philippoteau (1814–1880). He was not born when the battle took place, but painted this picture many years later.

UNIT 7

Napoleon

France in 1799

On 10 November, 1799 (19 Brumaire by the Revolutionary Calendar) there was uproar in the hall where members of the French government were meeting. After furious arguments, soldiers hustled many politicians out of the building, at bayonet-point (see Source 1). The troops were loyal to a young man called Napoleon Bonaparte, commander-in-chief of the army in Paris. A few weeks later, the Assembly was dissolved and a new government was installed, with Napoleon as leader. Suddenly, the Revolution was over. Why, and how, had this happened?

To answer this question, we need to look at France in 1799. How had the nation and its people been affected by ten years of revolutionary rule? Were the people really happier than they had been before the Revolution began? We also need to look at how rival groups of politicians felt in 1799, and why, once again, there were calls for the government to change.

AIMS

In this unit we shall look at the situation in France in 1799, ten years after the start of the Revolution. We will see who had gained, and who had lost, as a result of the revolutionary changes.

Next, we will look at the fascinating life story of Napoleon Bonaparte. He rose from humble beginnings as a young army officer to become Emperor of France. At the peak of his career it seemed that he would soon be master of all Europe too.

SOURCE 1
Napoleon seizes power, November 1799. A painting by François Bouchot (1800-1842).

Changes 1789 to 1799

The State

- No longer any king or royal family, ruling by inherited power. Now politicians are in control of France. They claim to rule 'for the people' but squabble among themselves.

- Government (national assembly) chosen by the people – all active citizens (see page 80) can vote. But between 1789 and 1799 many people were too frightened or confused to vote. Different groups of politicians seized control of the assembly at different times.

- Laws are made by national assembly, not by the king or his ministers. Powers of local *parlements* have been abolished.

- Old privileges (belonging to the king and the nobles) have also been abolished. Everyone is now equal in the eyes of the law.

The Economy

- Seriously weakened by the Revolution.

SOURCE 2
Bordeaux harbour – the Revolution disrupted trade and industry and caused problems for commercial cities such as this.

Cost of living:
This rose by 400 per cent between 1789 and 1797. Wages did not rise as quickly and many people went hungry.

Trade:
Overseas trade – the most profitable business before the Revolution (see Source 2) – now made up only 7 per cent of the French economy, instead of 25 per cent. Merchants and shopkeepers grew poorer.

Unemployment:
Rose rapidly; for example, in Bayeux, in 1787, the nobles and clergy employed 467 servants; in 1796 they employed 76. In Lyon, 50 per cent of the silk workshops closed down between 1789 and 1799.

Education

- Revolutionary governments planned to provide state education for everyone, but schools were never set up.
- Education was no longer to be controlled by the Roman Catholic Church.
- 50,000 pupils were attending colleges in 1789. Only 12,000 or 14,000 were attending central schools 10 years later. Basic literacy in France fell from 37 per cent in 1789 to around 30 per cent in 1815.

The Church

'We see lawful ministers, ... exiled from their homeland ... separated from their flocks. (We see) ... monks hounded out; holy virgins (nuns) without refuge; colleges and schools without the resources to live; churches ... dirty and in ruins ... in a word, a soulless, bloodless, powerless skeleton.'

SOURCE 3
Comment by an Italian church official, looking back in 1802.

- Church no longer a major property-owner. Church lands had been sold to raise money for the state.
- Tithes (tax to support the church) abolished. Church expenses and priests' wages now paid by the state.
- Bishops and other senior church officials now appointed by the state, not by the Pope.
- Freedom of religion – people were not penalised any more if they were not Roman Catholic.
- Church now has no money to give as charity. Before the Revolution it provided money, schools and hospitals for poor people.

NAPOLEON

The people

Who lost and who gained as a result of the French Revolution? The answers to this question might surprise you.

Nobles

Losses:
The nobility lost their titles and their old privileges. A few also had their property destroyed in the Revolution (see Source 4). Others left their estates and fled abroad.

Gains:
Most nobles stayed in France and some played an important part in Revolutionary politics. Many profited from the Revolution. They enlarged their estates by purchasing lands which had belonged to the Church and were then taken over and sold by the State. Some nobles were given jobs by the government.

SOURCE 5
The Revolution did not change agriculture. Peasants still farmed in old-fashioned ways and were very poor.

The bourgeoisie

Losses:
Some bourgeois lost their places in the old *parlements*. Some lost money because their wages did not keep pace with rising food prices.

Gains:
Wealthy bourgeois were able to purchase Church lands. Those who were educated as well as wealthy were given new jobs in state administration. Many members of the bourgeoisie – rich and poor – played an important part in Revolutionary politics.

Peasants

Losses:
Most poor people were poorer than before (see Source 5), because they no longer received charity from the church. In many parts of France new taxes were higher than pre-revolutionary ones, so peasants were worse off. Their wages did not keep pace with rising prices, so many went hungry. Men were forced to join the army and thousands were killed in battle.

Gains:
Feudal privileges were abolished, but this did not make very much difference politically or economically. A few rich peasants could vote.

SOURCE 4
Peasants attack nobles' estates, 1789.

ACTIVITY

'A strong leader is a good leader'.
Discuss this statement in a small group. Think of other examples of leaders in the past that you know of. Share your group's view with the rest of your class.

NAPOLEON

SOURCE 6
Popular print showing a revolutionary citizen, encouraged by his wife and family, setting off to join the army.

> 'The Revolutionaries have killed our king, driven away our priests and sold all the goods that belonged to our churches. They have eaten all our food, and now they want our bodies, too... They won't get them.'

SOURCE 8
Comment by anti-revolutionary peasant from the Vendée district of western France.

> 'The young men shall go to battle; husbands shall make and transport provisions; women shall sew (soldiers') clothes and tents, and serve in the hospitals; children shall turn old linen into bandages, and old men shall go out into the public squares to rouse the courage of the fighters, and to preach the unity of the republic and the hatred of kings.'

SOURCE 7
The duties of French citizens in wartime, set out in a revolutionary decree (order) of 1793.

France in crisis again?

The situation in 1799 reminded many French people of the crisis that had led to the Revolution breaking out in 1789. Prices were high, and many people could not afford to buy food. Peasants were rioting. The government was in debt, and the nation's leaders did not know how to solve France's economic problems. In Italy, the army was facing defeat. In Paris, politicians were divided into rival factions.

Takeover

When the republicans invited Napoleon to support their plans, they did not think that he would get involved in day-to-day politics. They assumed he would concentrate on the army, and on his military career. Instead, he seized complete control. In the rest of this unit we will look at how Napoleon ruled France. But first we must look at the army that helped him rise to power.

The people's army

In 1799, France was at war with almost all of Europe. For the first time, France was fighting with a 'citizen army'. At first, many French men and women were eager to fight for their country and the Revolution (see Source 6). But, as we can see from Source 7, warfare required an enormous effort and led to the sacrifice of hundreds of thousands of lives. It is not surprising that more and more ordinary men and women came to agree with the peasant quoted in Source 8.

Civil Rights

The events of the Revolution also brought greater freedom to women and non-Catholics though it did not make them more prosperous. Protestants and Jews could now worship freely. New laws on marriage and divorce were passed which meant that women now had greater control over this important area of their lives.

1. Why did the French people welcome Napoleon?
2. Which group of people was likely to welcome him most?

Napoleon's rise to power

Napoleon Bonaparte was born on the Mediterranean island of Corsica in 1769. For centuries, Corsica had been ruled by Italy. It was sold to France in 1768. Napoleon's family was poor, but ranked as nobility. It was active in local politics, and in the Corsican nationalist movement that grew up after France took over.

Having noble blood qualified Napoleon to enter an exclusive boarding school at Brienne, in France, when he was nine years old. He then trained at a leading army college in Paris. He studied hard and got good reports. However, there was nothing in Napoleon's family background or his schooling to suggest the enormous impact that he would later have on France, and on the whole of Europe.

Historians have described Napoleon's career as a 'thunderbolt' or a 'shooting star', because of his sudden and dramatic success. He ended the Revolution, and took control of the government, in an amazingly short time. On these two pages, you can see some of the stages in his astonishing rise to power. In the rest of this unit, you can see what Napoleon did when he ruled France.

SOURCE 9
'Napoleon crossing the Alps', a painting of Napoleon as a young man by David.

He prefers study to any kind of conversation, and nourishes his mind on good authors. He is moody, overbearing, self-centred. Though he speaks little, his replies are decisive and to the point . . . (He has) much self-love and boundless ambition.

SOURCE 10
Napoleon's report from army cadet school.

In 1791, Napoleon joins the Jacobin club. He eagerly supports its plans for reform. But after Robespierre's execution, all Jacobins are suspected, and the army commanders ask, is Napoleon really loyal? For a short time, he is imprisoned, but is soon set free. In October 1795, Napoleon proves his loyalty by helping to command the Parisian troops which put down the royalist rebellion of 13 Vendémiaire.

As a reward for his bravery, Napoleon is promoted. He is made commander of the army in Italy, where French armies are facing defeat. This is a great opportunity.

SOURCE 11
Josephine Beauharnais, a nobleman's widow. Napoleon married her in 1796.

On campaign in Italy, Napoleon soon wins brilliant victories, even though his troops are ragged and poorly-trained. He conquers all northern Italy, 1796-97.

Soldiers, you are naked (and) badly fed . . . Rich provinces and great towns will be in your power, and in them you will find honour, glory, wealth, Soldiers of (France in) Italy, will you be wanting in courage and steadfastness?

SOURCE 12
Napoleon's announcement to his troops, 1796.

NAPOLEON

Napoleon becomes a hero in France. The Directory is grateful to him for restoring French confidence. However, a few politicians remember Robespierre:

'Be on the lookout against the leaders of the army... a strong citizen might one day take over, and run the government.'

SOURCE 14
Remark by Robespierre, made early in the Revolution.

SOURCE 15
The coup d'état of November 1799, when Napoleon seized power.

After taking control of northern Italy, Napoleon and his troops advance on the Austrian capital of Vienna. The Austrians are forced to agree to a humiliating peace treaty at Campo Formio in 1797.

Napoleon – and the Directory – have great ambitions. If they can conquer Italy, why not advance further east, and win control of the entire Mediterranean sea? In 1798, Napoleon sets sail for Egypt. The same year, he wins an impressive victory against the Egyptians at the Battle of the Pyramids. But soon after, his fleet is destroyed by the British at the Battle of the Nile.

At home in France, Napoleon finds the country in crisis. The economy is in a mess, and people are discontented. The Directory seems powerless to help. On 19 Brumaire, with the help of his brother Lucien, he seizes power in a COUP D'ETAT.

There is bad news from home. Napoleon hears that his wife, Josephine (who was feeling neglected while he was away) is having an affair with a young army officer. Worse still, the French army has been badly defeated by Russian troops in Italy, and the Austrians are planning an attack. In October 1799, Napoleon hurries back to France.

SOURCE 13
British cartoon showing Napoleon and his troops looting art treasures from wealthy homes in Italy, 1796.

Inspired by the hope of winning further glory, Napoleon invades Syria in 1798 and 1799.

NAPOLEON

SOURCE 16
Napoleon as First Consul, 1799, painted by Baron Gros (1771–1835).

Rebuilding France

Napoleon was appointed First CONSUL (out of three) in 1799 (see Source 16). Although the three Consuls were meant to share power, it was obvious from the start that he was the real leader. Like the revolutionary governments before them, the Consuls summoned National Assemblies to share in government. But, unlike the revolutionary assemblies, they had no power. Napoleon kept all that for himself.

Strong government

Napoleon had clear ideas about what he wanted for France. At home, he aimed for strong government and an end to the uncertainties of the revolutionary years. However, there was a price to pay for this: Napoleon didn't like being criticised. He shut down newspapers that disagreed with him.

> 'I want peace, as much to settle the present French government, as to save the world from chaos.'

SOURCE 17
Comment by Napoleon to a Prussian diplomat, 1800.

Old ideas

In 1800, Napoleon and his officials introduced a new constitution, or statement of how France should be governed. His first aim was peace (see Source 17). He needed to end the revolutionary wars so that there would be time and money for rebuilding France. Napoleon's constitution announced that the Revolution was over, but it did maintain a few revolutionary policies. It was anti-royal, and it kept the state separate from the Church. However, Napoleon did not want Church and state to be at war, as they had been in revolutionary times. In 1802 he signed a CONCORDAT (agreement) with the Pope.

SOURCE 18
The new law-code, introduced by Napoleon in 1804.

1. Why did Napoleon reorganise French local government? Give at least two reasons.

2. Which of Napoleon's reforms do you think was most important? Explain your answer.

3. Some of Napoleon's new laws seemed necessary. Some were a result of his own views and political opinions about things. Give an example of each.

NAPOLEON

New institutions

Most historians agree that Napoleon's greatest achievement was the way in which he re-built the French government administration. Within a surprisingly short time, he introduced many changes. Some of the most important were:

- a new system of laws, the Code Napoleon (see Source 18).
- new state-run schools and colleges which he hoped would train the most intelligent people for government service (see Source 19).
- the first National Curriculum.
- 83 PRÉFETS were appointed – these were powerful officials chosen by, and obedient to, the central government (see Source 20). They were put in charge of *départements* (local government regions, rather like English counties), in place of locally elected officials.
- a centralised civil service.
- a new police network (complete with spies).
- a national bank.
- a special 'Legion of Honour' to reward people who had given outstanding service to France.

Without Napoleon's energy, enthusiasm and strong-arm tactics (he imprisoned over 2,500 opponents without trial), none of this would have happened.

SOURCE 20
Nineteenth century painting, showing a *préfet* wearing the special uniform designed when Napoleon was in power.

> Be honest and hard-working girls, tender and modest wives and wise mothers, and you will be good patriots. True patriotism consists in fulfilling one's duties and valuing only rights appropriate to each according to sex and age, and not wearing the cap of liberty and pantaloons and not carrying a pike and pistol. Leave those to men who are born to protect you and make you happy.

SOURCE 21
Advice to young girls written by a revolutionary journalist in 1793, and repeated by Napoleon.

Napoleon inherited many experimental reforms from the revolutionary period. He kept decimal coinage, and metric weights and measures, but he abolished the revolutionary calendar. Some of Napoleon's new laws came from pre-revolutionary times. Although he promised never to bring back feudal privileges, he restored nobles titles, and created many new titles himself. Like so many of his actions, this was carefully calculated to win political support.

Napoleon also abolished the revolutionary laws which gave greater freedom to women. Source 21 suggests that he saw 'liberated' women as a danger to political peace.

SOURCE 19
Pupils in a French LYCÉE (secondary school) today.

NAPOLEON

Master of Europe

From his early years in the army, Napoleon made no secret of his ambition to reach the top. If this helped France that would be good, but personal success was his main aim.

Even Napoleon's friends and close colleagues were sometimes surprised at just how much power and glory he wanted. As First Consul, he was sole ruler of France, but that was not enough (see Source 22). In 1804 he crowned himself Emperor. The Pope was at the ceremony, to give his blessing, but Napoleon was careful to place the crown on his head with his own hands. He wanted to make it clear that he owed his new position as Emperor to his own achievements. Source 23 shows a picture of this ceremony, painted after the event.

Many citizens were shocked when Napoleon divorced his wife because she was too old to have children. He was desperate for a son to follow him as Emperor, and so, when he was 40, he married the 18-year-old Austrian princess, Marie-Louise (Source 24). He made his four brothers 'kings' of conquered lands, and himself King of Italy. His mother became 'Madame Mère', a respectful title rather like 'Queen Mother'. When Napoleon's new wife gave birth to a son in 1811, the baby was proclaimed King of Rome. Less than 25 years after the Revolution, France now had a new 'royal family'.

Ambitions abroad

An emperor has to have an empire – a vast territory – to rule, so Napoleon set about conquering one. His motives were not simply ambition and greed. He genuinely wanted to protect France from its enemies, and to win new riches to restore its economy shattered by the Revolution. You can see a map of Napoleon's wars on page 107. On page 106 are details of his most important battles.

Napoleon as general

Napoleon had first come to power through his military skills, and it seems clear that he was a brilliant war leader. He enjoyed war, and found it interesting. He knew how to inspire his soldiers, and make them fight well. Even Napoleon's enemies admired his skills (see Source 25).

SOURCE 23
Napoleon crowns himself Emperor of France on 2 December 1804. A propaganda painting by Jacques-Louis David, who did not witness the scene, but painted it according to Napoleon's instructions.

> 'When I see an empty throne, I feel an urge to sit on it.'

SOURCE 22
Remark made by Napoleon in the early years of his rule.

attainment target

1 What can you tell about Napoleon from Source 22?
2 What can you tell about Napoleon's personality from Sources 22, 23 and 25?
3 How useful is Source 23 for telling us about Napoleon's coronation?
4 Source 23 is not accurate – how could historians make use of it anyway?

NAPOLEON

On the battlefield. Napoleon used traditional hand-to-hand fighting but with 'extras' – such as squads of sharpshooters who ran in front of his soldiers as they marched into battle, firing at the enemy before they were ready to fight back. He made quick decisions, and managed to get his troops quickly to the right place at the right time. He also made good use of cannon. These were deadly new weapons. Source 26 shows a typical Napoleonic battlefield at Eylau in 1807.

Child of the devil?

Napoleon was not always admired. Many people hated and feared him. They felt that while he lived, there would never be peace in Europe. Even his generals were revolted by his cold-blooded attitude to warfare. He enjoyed the sight of a battlefield littered with bodies and once said, 'The corpse of a dead enemy always smells good.' In France, there were plots to assassinate him in 1800, 1804 and 1812. Source 27 shows a cartoon, produced by his enemies, suggesting that Napoleon's behaviour was so 'inhuman' that he could only have learned it from the devil.

SOURCE 24
Marie-Louise of Austria, Napoleon's second wife, with their child, the King of Rome (born 1811).

> 'I used to say of him that his presence on the (battle) field made the difference of forty thousand men.'

SOURCE 25
Comment by the great British military commander, the Duke of Wellington, Napoleon's enemy.

SOURCE 26
Napoleon on the battlefield of Eylau, 1807.

Das ist mein lieber Sohn, an dem ich Wohlgefallen habe

SOURCE 27
Popular cartoon, showing Napoleon as the devil's child. Contrast this with Source 24.

NAPOLEON

Napoleon's wars 1800–1814

As we saw on pages 100–101, Napoleon had achieved great success leading French troops to victory in Italy. He had also used French military strength to negotiate a treaty at Campo Formio, in 1797, with Austria, France's powerful enemy. Now, in 1804, as Emperor of France, he planned once again to lead a French *Grande Armée* in battle against the great nations of Europe. Did he perhaps dream of one day becoming Emperor of Europe, as well? His most famous battles were:

1. Marengo 1800

176,000 French troops defeated Austrians and regained control of northern Italy. Napoleon almost lost this battle. If he had done, he might not have aimed to become Emperor of Europe.

2. Ulm 1805

French invasion force of almost 180,000, heading for Austria, defeated the Austrian army (33,000 men) at Ulm – the 'easiest victory'. Napoleon marches on.

3. Austerlitz 1805

Austrians re-gathered, and were supported by Russian allies, a total of 82,000 men. Napoleon and his soldiers advanced towards the Austrian capital. The two sides met; although the French army was smaller – around 65,000 – Austria and Russia were crushingly defeated. 20,000 men were killed or seriously wounded, and 15,000 were captured. France took over many countries ruled by Austria, including Belgium and the Netherlands.

4. Jena 1806

Prussia disliked Napoleon. Demanded that French troops, which had been occupying nearby German-speaking lands since the battle of Ulm, were withdrawn. In return, Napoleon declared war. The two sides met at Jena. Prussia was defeated. France took over many Prussian lands. A second battle was fought soon afterwards, at Auerstadt. 45,000 Prussian troops were scattered by a French army of only 26,000 men. In a single day, Napoleon had defeated Europe's most powerful kingdom.

5. Friedland 1807

Russian troops advanced towards France, through Poland. Napoleon hurried to attack. After fighting one battle against 80,000 Russians (at Eylau) in a snowstorm, his men faced a second Russian force. By a clever manoeuvre, Napoleon won victory. The Russians were massacred. 15,000 French were also killed. Napoleon then met the Russian Tsar Alexander, to discuss peace. They agreed the Treaty of Tilsit later in 1807.

6. Wagram 1809

Fought during Napoleon's second invasion of Austria. After a French defeat six weeks earlier at Aspern, near Vienna, Napoleon decided that he had to demonstrate new strength. He ordered the entire French army to march to Austria. Sheer weight of numbers (187,000 men and 500 cannon) caused the Austrians to retreat. As one historian has written, Wagram 'impressed Europe more than any earlier battle. Where previously there had been the hope that, with improved generalship and a bit of luck, Napoleon could be beaten, now it seemed as if his energy, his ruthlessness and his big battalions would carry him over any obstacle.'

7. Borodino 1812

Tsar Alexander of Russia wanted to trade peacefully with Britain. Napoleon wanted to stop this friendship between enemies of France, so he invaded Russia. At first, things went well. His army of 150,000 crushed the Russians at Borodino, although over a quarter (40,000) of his men were killed. Napoleon set off for Moscow but disaster struck. You can read more about Napoleon's Russian campaign on pages 110 and 111.

8. Leipzig 1813

Called the 'Battle of the Nations' because almost all Napoleon's enemies – Austria, Prussia, Russia, Britain, Sweden – joined together in a vast army (200,000 men) to fight him. They won. It showed, for the first time, that Napoleon could be defeated. It marked the beginning of the end of Napoleon's power.

NAPOLEON

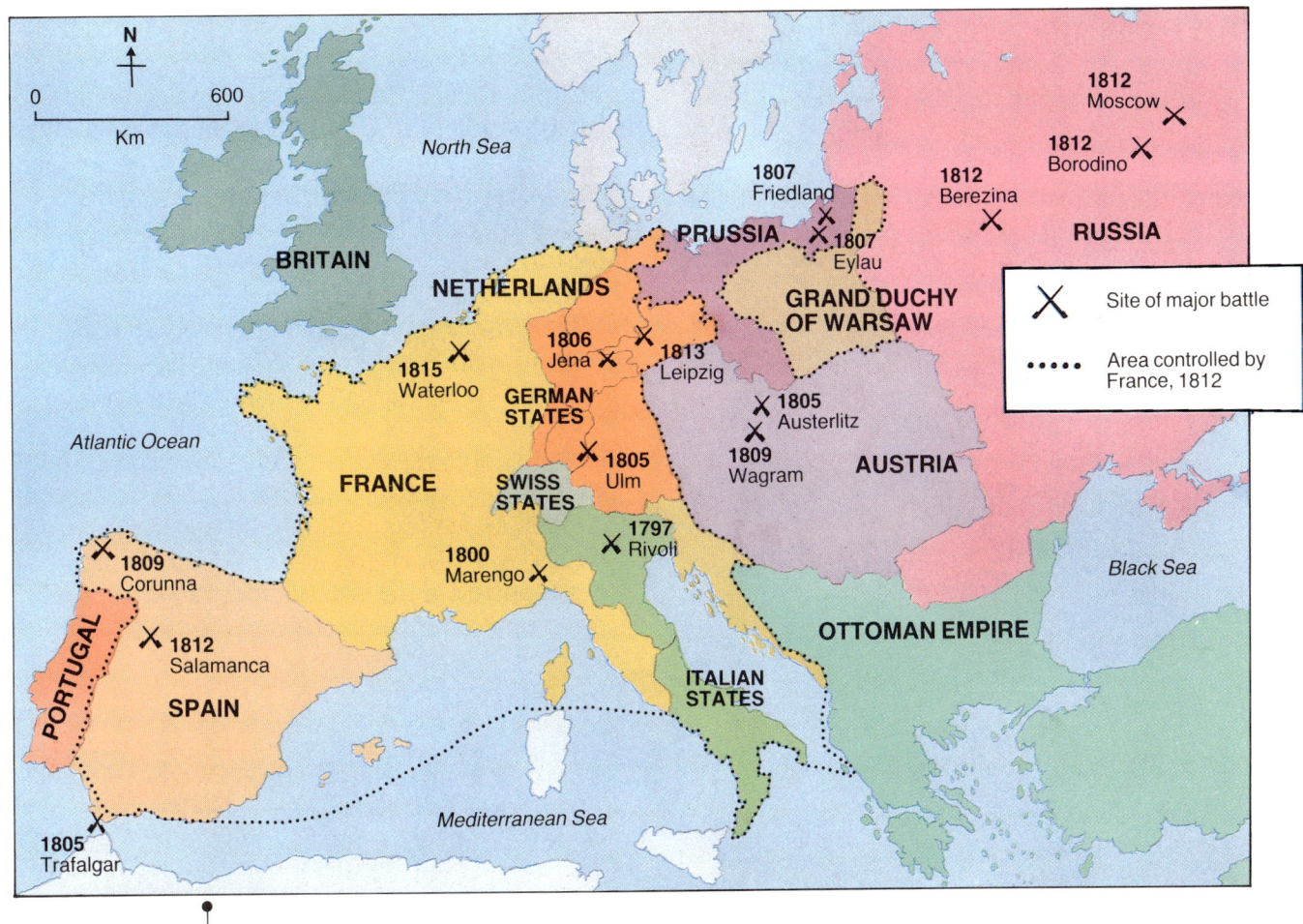

SOURCE 28 The locations of Napoleon's major battles.

Rival powers in Napoleon's Europe

France

Ruled by Napoleon. After 1807, he controlled most of Europe. Made marriage alliance (1810) with former major enemy, Austria. Considering plans to invade the Middle East. Facing GUERRILLA rebels in Spain (see page 109) and hostility from Britain.

Austria, Prussia (north Germany), Russia

The largest and most powerful states in Eastern Europe. Napoleon's enemies, for most of his time in power. Previously, they had been at war with Revolutionary France. All defeated by Napoleon in battle. All forced to give up large areas of land. They feared that all Europe would soon be ruled by Napoleon and his family – he made his brothers and sister rulers of their newly-conquered lands.

Germany and Italy

Not the same as present-day countries with the same name. Before Napoleon, ruled by many independent princes and controlled by (or allied to) Austria, Prussia and Russia. Invaded by Napoleon's armies and, after 1807, controlled by France. Men from conquered lands were forced to fight in the French army. They hated this.

Great Britain

Had been at war with France for much of the 18th century. Like Austria, Prussia and Russia, opposed Revolutionary ideas. Now was preparing to defend itself against invasion by Napoleon's troops (see pages 108 and 109).

Spain and Portugal

Allies of Britain. Invaded by France in 1807 (Portugal) and 1808 (Spain) (see page 109).

NAPOLEON

Old enemies

England and France had been enemies for many years before Napoleon came to power. At first, some British politicians and writers welcomed the French Revolution. However, most people in Britain were horrified by the execution of Louis XVI and by the violence and bloodshed during the Terror.

As Napoleon seized more and more power, British leaders began to think it was their duty to defend the world against him. Cartoons like Source 29 were published, to spread these views.

War at sea

In 1798, French troops led by Napoleon defeated British soldiers at Aboukir Bay, in Egypt. But a few weeks later, at the Battle of the Nile, English ships destroyed France's Mediterranean fleet, and wrecked Napoleon's bid to gain power in the Middle East.

War broke out once more in 1803, when Napoleon's troops occupied the Netherlands, Britain's ally. Soon afterwards, in 1804, Napoleon planned an invasion of Britain. This failed, because of bad weather, bad planning and bad luck. In 1805, the British navy, commanded by Nelson (see Source 30) hit back. They destroyed 20 French warships sailing off Cape Trafalgar (see Source 31), on the coast of Spain. Britain now controlled the seas all around France, and Napoleon never tried to fight at sea again.

SOURCE 29
Cartoon, showing Napoleon as a greedy spider, by the English artist Thomas Rowlandson (1756–1827).

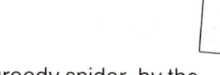

SOURCE 30
Admiral Lord Nelson and his fellow navy commanders plan their battle against Napoleon on board ship.

SOURCE 31
The battle of Trafalgar, 1805.

NAPOLEON

SOURCE 32
Arthur Wellesley, Duke of Wellington (1769–1852). A portrait by the Spanish artist Francisco Goya.

> **attainment target**
>
> Here are three different descriptions of Napoleon, written by modern historians:
>
> - 'a military genius'
> - 'he was chiefly interested in power'
> - '(his) violence . . . bred hatred and fear, and (his) trickery destroyed all trust'.
>
> 1 Which of these views do you think is more accurate? Explain your choice and compare it with the others.
>
> 2 Why do you think there are such differing views of Napoleon?

The 'Continental System'

After Trafalgar, Napoleon decided to use a different weapon against Britain. He forbade all French people – and people in all lands conquered by France – to buy British goods, or goods from British colonies. He hoped an 'economic war' would ruin the 'nation of shopkeepers', as he scornfully called Britain. He also hoped that this economic war – known as the CONTINENTAL SYSTEM – would strengthen the French economy, as most of Europe would be forced to buy French goods instead.

His plan did not succeed. Smuggling was widespread and people in conquered lands did all they could to break the trading rules.

The Peninsular War

Britain and France were soon fighting again. After Napoleon's troops invaded Portugal in 1807 and Spain in 1808, these two countries (known as the Iberian Peninsula) became a battleground. The Spanish people rebelled against French government, and asked Britain to help them fight.

SOURCE 33
Spanish guerrillas making bullets.

Britain sent rather rough and ready troops, but they were led by two brilliant generals, Arthur Wellesley (later Duke of Wellington, shown in Source 32) and Sir John Moore.

The rugged Spanish landscape, and the TERRORIST tactics used by Spanish freedom fighters meant that, for once, Napoleon could not win. The freedom fighters were known as guerrillas (see Source 33). They would not give in even when French soldiers used brutal punishments. After Britain won important battles at Salamanca in 1812 and at Vitoria in 1813, the French had to retreat. The Peninsula was free.

NAPOLEON

A fatal mistake

In 1810, France controlled almost all Europe. Only Britain, Russia and Portugal remained free. In 1810, Tsar Alexander, shown in Source 34, announced that he was going to ignore Napoleon's 'Continental System' and start trading with Britain again. Napoleon was angry and alarmed. If Britain and Russia became friends, they could defeat France (see Source 35).

Napoleon decided to invade Russia. He planned to give the Tsar a 'short, sharp shock', by attacking Russia with an enormous army, winning a few quick victories, and then marching home. Napoleon hoped he would be able to force the Tsar to abandon his friendship with Britain. Then France would be supreme.

SOURCE 35
British cartoon, glorifying Russian strength.

SOURCE 34
Tsar Alexander of Russia (1777–1825).

1 List two short-term and two long-term consequences of Napoleon's attack on Russia.

2 What do you think might have happened if Napoleon had invaded Russia in summertime?

3 What does Napoleon's Russian campaign tell us about (a) his character? (b) his attitude towards his soldiers? (c) his political ambitions?

SOURCE 36
Napoleon's Russian campaign, 1812.

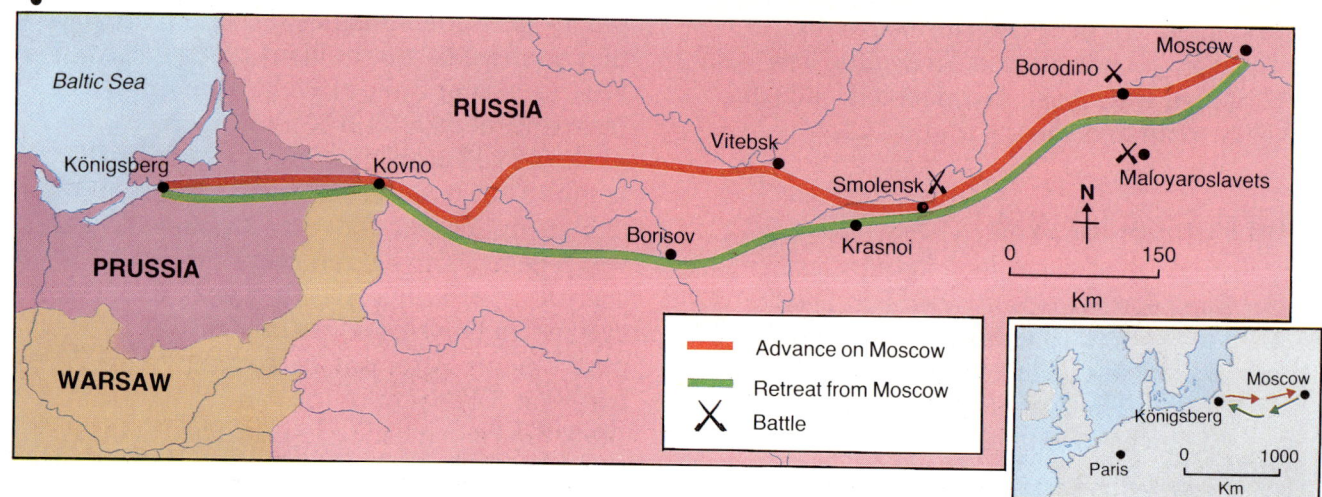

A massive attack

Napoleon's plans went disastrously wrong. In 1812, he assembled a vast army on the border between Poland and Russia. He hoped to overpower the Russians by sheer weight of numbers. But the Russians refused to fight. Instead, they retreated towards Moscow. Napoleon's troops were forced to chase them through harsh, hostile territory (the route of their long journey is shown in Source 36). Food ran short; Napoleon hoped for a brief campaign, so he had only arranged supplies for three weeks. The two sides fought at Borodino, about 110 kilometres from Moscow. The French won the battle, but the Russians would not admit defeat. Napoleon led his armies onwards to Moscow. The Russians set fire to the city (Source 37) in an attempt to thwart the French. Tsar Alexander still would not surrender; he knew that, in spite of their seeming success, Napoleon and his men were trapped.

Failure

Napoleon was forced to abandon his attack on Moscow in October 1812. His men were exhausted, cold and hungry (see Source 38). The bitter Russian winter was just beginning – soon, heavy snow would fall, and the temperature would remain below freezing point all day long. He was 2,400 kilometres from Paris, and surrounded by enemies. He had stopped trying to make Tsar Alexander give in. Now his task was to try to get his men home.

'General Winter'

Napoleon was defeated by the problems of moving an army vast distances across Russian territory, and, most of all, by the Russian weather. 'General Winter' had succeeded where human army commanders had failed. 'He' had conquered Napoleon (see Source 39). Europe's mightiest army perished from cold, hunger and disease.

At home in France, people were horrified. They mourned the dead soldiers and plotted to remove Napoleon from power. News of the disastrous retreat from Moscow echoed all round Europe. The invasion of Russia had been a fatal mistake. Napoleon's army lost 570,000 men there as well as 200,000 horses and 1,100 cannon. People began to say that the French empire – and its Emperor – were not so great as they appeared.

SOURCE 38
French soldiers suffered terribly on the retreat from Moscow in the winter of 1812–1813.

SOURCE 37
Moscow in flames, being attacked by Napoleon's troops.

'Russia has two generals she can trust – Generals January and February.'

SOURCE 39
Remark made by Tsar Nicholas I, who ruled Russia later in the 19th century, looking back at 1813.

NAPOLEON

From hero to villain

SOURCE 40
Napoleon in IMPERIAL robes, painted by François-Pascal Gérard.

SOURCE 41
Napoleon faces death at the battle of Leipzig. A British cartoon of 1813.

ACTIVITY

Make a wall display on the topic of 'heroes', from the present-day and from the past. Write captions to explain why you have chosen each man or woman.

Sources 40 and 41 present two contrasting images of Napoleon. Source 40 shows a picture of him as Emperor which he ordered to be painted when he was at the height of his power. Source 41 shows a cartoon of Napoleon drawn by a British artist in 1813. As Napoleon himself said, 'From the sublime to the ridiculous. There is only one step.'

The cartoon in Source 41 was published after Napoleon had been crushingly defeated at Leipzig by an alliance of his enemies. In 1814, France faced invading armies sent from Britain, Austria and Prussia. Napoleon also faced enemies at home; Source 42 records just some of their complaints. Many French people felt that war was tragic even when they were victorious. Now they were defeated, the waste of lives and money seemed inexcusable.

> Our ills are at their height. The homeland is threatened at all points of the frontier; we are suffering from poverty and wretchedness unexampled in the whole history of the state. Commerce is destroyed, industry dying... What are the causes of these unspeakable miseries? A troublesome administration, too many taxes, dreadful methods adopted to collect them, and even crueller schemes to recruit the armies... A barbaric and endless war swallows up... youth torn from education, agriculture, commerce and the arts...

SOURCE 42
Complaint by members of Napoleon's government, 1813.

Giving up power

In 1814, Paris was captured by allied troops. Napoleon now had no choice – he had to abdicate. Source 43 shows an emotional moment – Napoleon saying farewell to his army. The invading allies sent Napoleon into exile on the tiny Mediterranean island of Elba. He was given a royal title, but he no longer had any power. In future, the invaders decided, France was to be ruled once more by a king. They invited the oldest surviving brother of Louis XVI to reign. He took the title of Louis XVIII, and was crowned later that year.

NAPOLEON

SOURCE 43
Napoleon saying farewell to his troops, 1814.

'A battle of giants.'

SOURCE 44
Contemporary comment on the battle of Waterloo.

'The nearest-run thing you ever saw in your life.'

SOURCE 45
Comment by the Duke of Wellington, commander of the British army at the battle of Waterloo.

The 'hundred days'

Napoleon did not like life in exile. He plotted to seize power once more. In 1815, he escaped from Elba, and sailed to the south of France. He marched towards Paris, attracting eager followers along the way. They hoped he would bring back France's greatness. King Louis XVIII escaped to Belgium, in terror.

Back in control, in Paris, Napoleon promised peace. He said he would govern France gently, according to the law. He also said he had given up his plans to conquer the whole of Europe, but many people did not believe him. They watched suspiciously while he began to recruit a new army. Just two months after Napoleon arrived in Paris, he led 150,000 men to invade Belgium. There, he fought British and Prussian troops, led by Wellington and Blücher, Europe's two best generals, at the battle of Waterloo (see Sources 44, 45 and 46). He was only just defeated (see Source 45), but that was enough to end his second chance as Emperor after only a hundred days. Napoleon was exiled again, this time to St Helena, an island in the South Atlantic. He died there, six years later, aged 52.

SOURCE 46
The battlefield at Waterloo, in Belgium. Painted many years afterwards by Sir William Allen (1803–1852).

MAKING CONNECTIONS

Cromwell and Napoleon

What makes a good leader? Is it their ability to inspire others to work for them, or what they actually achieve themselves? Do wartime leaders need to have different qualities from peacetime ones? Does personality matter? Should leaders be kind, honest, pleasant people, or can they be cruel, immoral and untrustworthy, so long as they get results? Does a man make a better leader than a woman? Should leaders be ambitious – for themselves or for their countries, or should they aim for a 'quiet life'? Should they rule with the consent of the people, or impose their will on them? Is their public image important. And does it matter whether they are liked and admired, hated or feared?

Two 'great' leaders?

Considering the answers to all these questions can help us compare two outstanding leaders – Oliver Cromwell (1599 to 1658) and Napoleon Bonaparte (1769 to 1821) – who both came to power after unpopular governments had been overthrown. Undoubtedly, both were very powerful men, who led their countries in difficult times. But what else about them was similar, and what was different?

'Truly his memory stinks.'
'The days of Oliver Cromwell were marvellous days of prosperity, freedom and peace.'

SOURCE 47
Two judgements on Oliver Cromwell: the first made by a Royalist, the second by a Puritan.

'The greatest of men in the greatest of nations.'
'Down with the tyrant.'

SOURCE 48
Two comments about Napoleon from 1814: the first made by a préfet (government official), the second shouted by an angry crowd in southern France.

ACTIVITY

Look at pages 45 to 49 (for Cromwell) and pages 94 to 113 (for Napoleon) to remind yourselves of their careers. You can also read the biographies on the opposite page. Sources 49 and 50 show portraits commissioned (specially ordered) by each ruler when they were at the height of their powers. Sources 47 and 48 give contrasting opinions of each man from people living at the time.

1 Use the Copy sheet 'Cromwell and Napoleon' from the Teacher's Notes and fill in as much information as you can for each leader.

2 When you have completed the Copy sheet, you will be able to compare the personalities, wartime achievements and political careers of Cromwell and Napoleon. You could use the following three criteria to decide which of them was the better leader:

- the success or failure of their policies
- the short-term effect of their policies on their countries
- the long-term effect of their policies on their countries.

3 These are useful comparisons but, to be fair, you should also consider another factor. What political, economic and military problems did Cromwell and Napoleon have to cope with when they first came to power? Who do you think faced the more difficult task? Look back at pages 44 to 47 (Cromwell) and pages 96 to 99 (Napoleon) to help you think about this.

MAKING CONNECTIONS

OLIVER CROMWELL

- **Oliver Cromwell** was born in 1599 in Huntingdon, the son of a farmer. He went to grammar school and Cambridge University.

- In 1620 he married Elizabeth Bourchier, daughter of a rich London merchant.

- He was a farmer and an MP in the Parliament of 1628 to 1629, a Puritan and opponent of Charles I, although not among the leaders. He was a backbench MP in the Parliament of 1640 and when the Civil War broke out in 1642 he organised Parliamentary forces in his area. Although he had no military training, he became the outstanding Parliamentary general of the Civil War. He led his 'Ironsides' to their first victory at Gainsborough in 1643 and at Marston Moor in 1644. He became Commander of the New Model Army in 1645 and defeated the King at Naseby.

- He defeated the Scots at Preston in 1648 and pressed for the execution of the King in 1649.

- In Ireland he ruthlessly ended the Civil War and massacred the royalist garrisons of Drogheda and Wexford in 1649.

- His willingness to promote soldiers on grounds of their military ability, rather than their social rank, and his tolerance of religious beliefs, made him the hero of the Army.

- You can read about his time as Lord Protector from 1653 on page 49.

SOURCE 49
Oliver Cromwell asked the artist to paint him 'warts and all'.

NAPOLEON BONAPARTE

- **Napoleon Bonaparte** was born on the island of Corsica in 1769, the son of a poor nobleman who was active in politics. After school in France he attended army training college.

- He was a Roman Catholic, but mistrusted the political power of the Church.

- He supported the Jacobins (radicals) during the French Revolution, and was briefly imprisoned. But after 1794, he supported the moderate Directory government and was rewarded by a promotion in the army.

- In 1796 he married Josephine Beauharnais, a nobleman's widow, related to senior army commanders. He was promoted again.

- From 1796–1798 he led French troops on a series of victorious campaigns in Italy, Austria and Egypt.

- In 1799 he took over the government and was in total control of France until 1814, as First Consul, and after 1804 as self-proclaimed emperor (see pages 102 to 107).

- Between 1804 and 1814 he led the French army in wars against many nations in Europe (see pages 106 to 111 for details).

- Napoleon wanted a male heir. Josephine was too old to have children so he divorced her to marry young princess Marie-Louise of Austria in 1810.

- In 1813, France was defeated at the battle of Leipzig. In 1814, France was invaded by an alliance of European states. Napoleon was exiled. A new French king, Louis XVIII, was crowned.

- In 1815, Napoleon escaped from exile and took over the French government once again. But he was defeated at the battle of Waterloo (1815), and sent back into exile, where he died, aged 52, in 1821.

SOURCE 50
Napoleon ordered this portrait shortly after he crowned himself emperor in 1804.

115

UNIT 8

A new Europe

AIMS

In this unit we will look at what happened to France and to the rest of Europe after Napoleon was driven from power. We will look, too, at the influence of the Revolution, and of Napoleon's empire, on fashions in art, design and ideas. Finally, we will ask, 'what is a revolution?'

After Napoleon

In 1815, the nations that had joined together to defeat Napoleon (Austria, Russia, Prussia and Britain) held a meeting – the Congress of Vienna (see Source 1). Now that Napoleon was safely out of the way, they had to make sure that no single individual ever threatened the peace of Europe again.

Far away on the island of St Helena, Napoleon's new life was very different and he was feeling homesick. He was also trying to persuade himself – and others – that the French people missed him (see Source 2). The leaders gathered at the Congress of Vienna were of a very different opinion. They did not want him back.

SOURCE 1
European government leaders meet at the Congress of Vienna, 1815.

'Millions of men weep for us, the homeland (France) sighs . . . the wishes of the nations are for us.'

SOURCE 2
Written by Napoleon while in exile on St Helena.

A NEW EUROPE

> 'A standing army of soldiers, a kneeling army of priests and a creeping army of officials.'

SOURCE 4
How Metternich's opponents described his new, backward-looking system of government.

SOURCE 3
New boundaries for European states drawn up at the Congress of Vienna.

SOURCE 5
King Louis XVIII (1755–1824) in royal robes. A painting by François-Louis Gérard.

New boundaries

Lands conquered by Napoleon were shared out among the allies who had defeated him (see Source 3). Contemporaries said that 'the map of Europe is being re-drawn'. Germany, Italy and Scandinavia were divided up. Belgium was given to the Netherlands. This policy soon proved disastrous. No-one considered the views of the many different ethnic groups living in those countries. Years later, there were riots and revolutions as nationalist groups sought independence for their homelands.

1. Why do you think the political boundaries drawn up at the Congress of Vienna did not last?
2. When he was an old man, Prince Metternich said that all his life had been spent 'trying to support decaying structures'. What do you think he meant by this?

Return to the past

What kind of government did the allies want to replace Napoleon? Basically, they wanted a return to the days before the Revolution. This would mean rule by kings and princes, a powerful Church, a strong army and an efficient civil service, all loyal to the king and his ministers. Free discussion, democratic elections and 'the will of the people' would not be allowed. The diplomats who persuaded European leaders to go back to these old ways were led by the conservative Prince Metternich of Austria. He had always been an enemy of the French Revolution. Some people disagreed or were critical of Metternich's 'reforms' (see Source 4). To them it looked as if all Europe would be kept under tight government control.

A new king

The allies also decided that there should, once again, be a king of France. Louis XVI's brother, Louis-Stanislas-Xavier, was next in line to the throne. He had already been welcomed by French royalists as King Louis XVIII, and, at Vienna, the allies agreed that he should remain the ruler of France. You can see the new King's portrait, painted to proclaim his royal splendour to all Europe, in Source 5.

A NEW EUROPE

Heritage of the Revolution

After Napoleon was sent into exile, Louis XVIII ruled as King of France. Opinions about King Louis varied. He was accused of being devious (not straightforward) and elitist (favouring the upper classes). His own comment (in Source 6) reveals his desire to 'turn back the clock' to the days of royal rule. But, unlike earlier kings, he respected the wishes of the people. His government preserved many of the revolutionary and Napoleonic reforms, and ruled strictly according to the 'Charter', introduced in 1814. This 'ruler's code' was based on constitutions drawn up by the Directory and in 1791.

Peace

There was one issue, however, on which everyone agreed. They wanted peace. Over 860,000 young French men (aged between 23 and 44) were killed in Napoleon's wars. Before that, another 40,000 French men and women had died during the Revolution. In towns, merchants and manufacturers wanted the chance to build new factories and re-establish trade. In the countryside, lawyers and estate-owners, noble families and peasants all wanted the chance to get on with their lives free from the threat of war. Source 7 shows the 'domestic' ideal, which many French families aimed for – tranquillity, comfort and content.

Shaping society

The wish for peace was one of the most important short-term effects of the Revolution and the Napoleonic era for French society. But there were other, longer-term consequences, as well. Even though the monarchy was restored, almost all the old government institutions had been swept away. Many important new ones – such as the Revolution's local government and Napoleon's education system – were now shaping French society, as they still do today.

The French nation did not forget its revolutionary heritage. The streets of Paris were ornamented with grand monuments such as the Eiffel Tower (see Source 8), commemorating revolutionary events. In many other towns, streets were re-named after revolutionary heroes or Napoleon's great victories. Even the fighting words of the Marseillaise, the French national anthem, (see Source 9), still remind French people of their nation's revolutionary past.

> **attainment target**
>
> Compare life in France in 1788 (as described in unit 5) with life in France in 1820. Look at the changes affecting all the different groups in French society – the royal family, the nobles, the clergy, the bourgeois and the peasants.
>
> 1 Whose life had changed the most?
>
> 2 Whose life had changed for the better and whose for the worse?

> Servant: 'Sire, now you are King of France.'
> Louis XVIII: 'When have I NOT been King?'

SOURCE 6
Remark made by Louis XVIII, when a servant congratulated him in 1814.

SOURCE 7
Mid-19th century painting of a comfortable bourgeois family in France. After the Revolution and Napoleon's reign many people hoped for peace and a quiet life at home.

A NEW EUROPE

Symbols of liberty

During the 19th century, there were several rebellions by the French people against governments which they believed to be unjust. In 1830, King Charles X, Louis XVI's youngest brother, was driven into exile. In 1848, a revolutionary commune ran Paris, turning another king, Louis-Philippe, off the throne. In all these upheavals, protesters were inspired by the 1789 Revolution. Romantic images of republican ideas, such as 'Liberty' were popular (see Source 10). The artists who painted romantic pictures hoped they would link all these later rebellions with the original Revolution, forming a 'Great Tradition' of revolutionary thought and action, and glorifying France, an inspiration to the world.

SOURCE 8
The famous Eiffel Tower, Paris, built in 1889 to commemorate the first centenary of the Revolution.

> The bloody flag of tyrannical government still waves above our heads. Can you hear, throughout the land, the shouts of the soldiers? Citizens, get your weapons! Organise your troops! March onwards, onwards! Let the poisoned blood of our enemies soak into our fields.

SOURCE 9
The first verse of the Marseillaise (translated).

SOURCE 10
Painting by Eugène Delacroix (1798–1863) called 'Liberty Leading the People'.

MAKING CONNECTIONS

Revolutions in history

The words in Source 11 were spoken by Gabriel Noël, a volunteer soldier in the revolutionary army, in 1792. Many French people, from wealthy deputies to poor citizens of Paris, shared Noël's hopes. They believed that revolutionary France was leading the way towards a new and better society, where freedom and equality would be guaranteed for all.

The French Revolution, and the years when Napoleon ruled, certainly did affect Europe, and, gradually, the rest of the world, as you can see from the timeline of revolutions on this page. These revolutions were inspired by French ideas of liberty and equality. They were also caused by a new, powerful spirit of nationalism (national pride and demands for independence). This grew as a reaction partly to Napoleon's plans for French conquests, and partly to the new national boundaries insensitively imposed at the Congress of Vienna in 1815.

'The spirit of liberty is going to envelop the entire world.'

SOURCE 11
Comment by a French revolutionary soldier, 1792.

Revolutions 1750-1850

Date	Place	Aims
1755	Corsica	Independence
1768	Geneva	Democracy
1773	South-east Russia	Independence
1775	America	Independence and democracy
1789	**France**	**Liberty and equality**
1789	Liège (Belgium)	Anti-feudalism
1790	Hungary	Independence
1791	Haiti	Anti-slavery
1791	Poland	Democracy and freedom
1793	Sardinia	Independence
1798	Ireland	Independence and religious freedom
1804	Serbia	Independence
1808	Spain	Anti-Napoleon/ Independence
1809	Austrian Tyrol	Anti-Napoleon/ Independence
1811-1829	Central and South America	Independence
1830	Greece	Independence
1830	Belgium	Independence
1831	Poland	Independence
1848-1849	Italy Germany Hungary	Independence

SOURCE 12
Garibaldi and his followers started a revolution to remove foreign rulers from Italy during the 19th century.

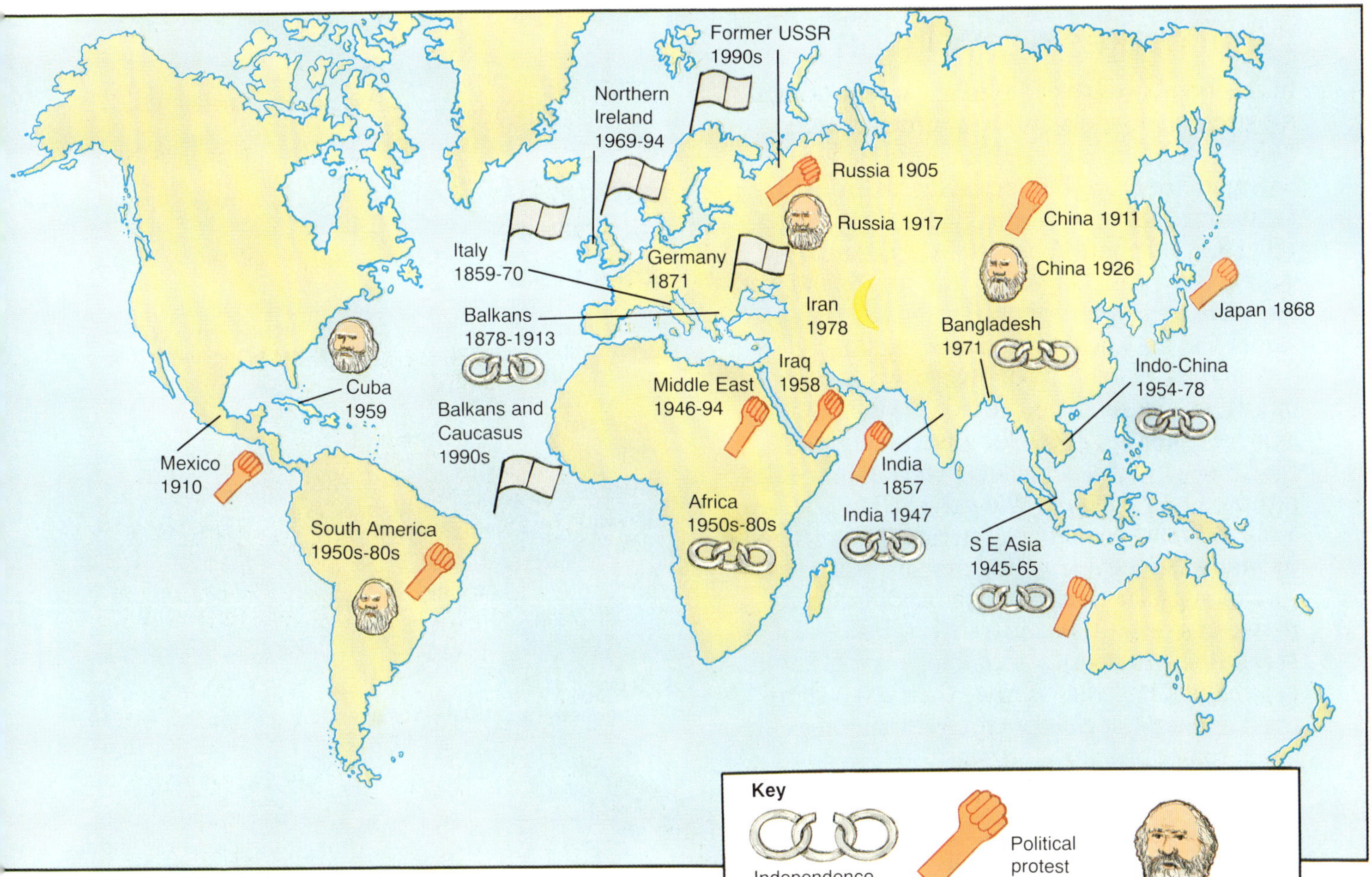

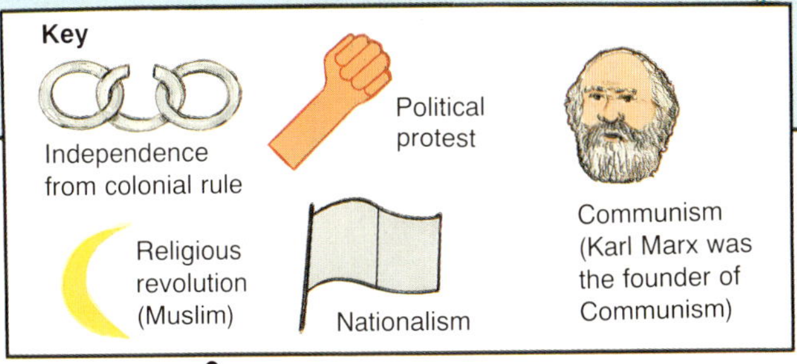

MAKING CONNECTIONS

SOURCE 13
Some major world revolutions from 1850 onwards.

Revolutionary inspiration

The French Revolution was just one of many revolutions that have happened in the past. Revolutionary politicians (see Sources 12 and 14) in later years have not all shared the same aims as revolutionary leaders in France. As you can see from Source 13, later revolutions have been sparked off by many different political grievances. Even so, the French Revolution has continued to inspire people in many parts of the world. It has shown that if ordinary citizens are prepared to take action, they can transform their nations and their lives.

1. Why do you think so many later revolutions were inspired by the French Revolution?
2. If you were a revolutionary leader, what do you think would be the most useful lesson you could learn from the French Revolution?
3. What mistakes (if any) made by French Revolutionary leaders would you try to avoid?

SOURCE 14
A Russian revolutionary poster, showing the leader, Lenin, who played an important part in the Russian Revolution of 1917. Painted 1917–1920.

MAKING CONNECTIONS

What makes a revolution?

In this book, we have looked at two episodes in the past when 'the world was turned upside down' (see Sources 15 and 16). New leaders emerged (for example, Source 17), to lead angry protesters. Countries were divided by rival religious and political beliefs. Many ordinary people were killed in rioting (Source 18) and war. But were these years of upheaval really the same? Did they lead to similar results?

You must think of your own answers to those questions, but most people would probably answer 'no'. After 1660, the government of England – and many English people's lives – returned to the old pre-war pattern. But after 1789 in France, society was permanently altered by new ideas, new laws and new institutions.

This suggests that there is a big difference between a revolution and a civil war. A revolution – in politics, technology, social habits or even just in style – is more than just a short-lived upheaval. It changes things, sometimes for good, sometimes for bad, but always for ever.

'We must never rest until all Europe is in flames.'

'Freedom will be ours for ever
We'll put an end to cruel tyrants...'

SOURCE 15
Two revolutionary slogans from France: the first, a comment by the journalist, Jacques-Pierre Brissot (1754–1793), the second, words from a popular song from 1789.

'Charles Stuart, King of England, trusted to govern according to the laws of the land, had a wicked design to create for himself an unlimited power to rule according to his will and to overthrow the rights and liberties of the people.'

SOURCE 16
The charge against King Charles at his trial in January 1649.

SOURCE 17
Statue of John Hampden in Aylesbury town centre.

SOURCE 18
Parisian women march to Versailles, October 1789.

1. Can you think of any 'revolutions' in fashion, sport, music, technology, or ideas?

2. Finish this sentence: 'A revolution is a time when...'

Glossary

Anarchy
Without government or laws.

Ancestors
People from whom we are descended; our parents, grandparents, great-grandparents, etc.

Anvil
A large iron block used by a blacksmith when hammering and shaping objects.

Architect
A person who designs buildings.

Assassination
The murder of an important politician or a monarch.

Assignats
Certificates issued by the revolutionary government in France, which came to be used as a form of paper money.

Banished
Punished by being sent out of the country in which you live.

Bourgeois
Living in a town.

Bourgeoisie
People (like lawyers and merchants) who lived in towns; an important group in French society.

Cahiers
Literally, notebooks; used to describe the lists of complaints made by people living in the provinces. They were discussed at the meeting of the Estates-General in 1789.

Capitation
French poll-tax.

Ceremony
The words or actions of a church service as set out in a prayer book.

Churchwardens
People in a parish who care for the local church's building, decoration and furniture.

Civil War
War among people of the same country.

Coffer
A chest used for storing money.

Concordat
An agreement or treaty.

Consul
A title for a leader of a republican government. It originated in Ancient Rome.

Continental system
Napoleon's scheme to try and make all France and all lands conquered by France boycott British-made goods. It failed.

Cope
A large cloak worn by a priest.

Corrupt
Dishonest and open to bribery.

Coup d'état
A sudden change of government, usually the result of force.

Customs
Money paid to the government when goods are taken in or out of a country.

Départements
Local government regions in France, rather like British counties. France was first divided into départements by the revolutionary government in 1791.

Deputies
Elected representatives, rather like Members of Parliament, who played an important part in the French revolutionary government.

Directory
The group of moderate French politicians who governed France after the Terror ended in 1794. They were driven out of office when Napoleon seized power in 1799.

Divine Right
The belief that kings or other heads of state are appointed by God. Usually believed only by kings, their ministers and leading church authorities. According to this belief, any criticism or rebellion might be viewed as a sin (since it went against God's choice) as well as a political crime.

Douanes
Customs duties paid on goods taken to market.

GLOSSARY

Dynasty
A succession of rulers from the same family.

Enclosure
Dividing up open fields by putting up fences or hedges across them.

Factions
Minority breakaway groups.

Feudal dues
Payments made to a land owner by peasants living on their land, in return for rights such as using the landowner's mill to grind their corn, or fishing in his or her rivers. They were deeply resented.

Feudalism
An ancient system of rights and privileges connected with landholding. Under the feudal system, a major landowner had the right to demand rent plus various other money payments and sometimes also work from the peasants who lived on his or her land.

Flogged
Whipped.

Gabelle
A tax on salt. Everyone had to pay this, since salt was used in cooking and for preserving food.

Galante
Elegant, graceful and light-hearted.

Girondins
A group of French revolutionary politicians, with outspoken, but not extremist, views. They quarrelled with the Jacobins over how much violence it was necessary to use against critics of the Revolution.

Guerrillas
Fighters who use surprise tactics, such as ambushes or hit-and-run raids, against their enemies, instead of fighting pitched battles.

Imperial
Belonging to an empire.

Incense
A substance used in religious ceremonies which burns with a sweet smell.

Jacobins
A group of French revolutionaries who believed that criticism of the Revolution was dangerous, and should be stopped by executing all opponents. They were responsible for 'The Terror' of 1793 to 1794.

Laboureurs
French peasants who were rich enough to own their own land.

Lease
An agreement between a landlord and a tenant laying out how much rent is to be paid, for how long, etc.

Lycée
French secondary school, which aimed to produce academically very successful pupils with well-trained minds. French secondary schools are still called lycées.

Massacre
The killing of a large number of defenceless people.

Merchandise
Goods for sale.

Métayers
French peasants who rented land from people wealthier than themselves. In return, they gave the landowner half of the crops or livestock they produced.

Minister
Someone who helps the monarch to rule.

Moderates
Politicians who supported the French Revolution, but did not want to see major changes happen too quickly, or with too much bloodshed.

Nationalism
Loyalty to a country and its territory, language and way of life. Usually combined with a wish for a political independence.

Pamphlet
A short printed booklet.

Parlements
French pre-revolutionary local law courts.

Popish
An insulting term for Roman Catholic.

Pre-revolutionary
Something that happened before a Revolution.

Préfets
French local government officials, each responsible for a département. Introduced by Napoleon.

Protestant
Someone who protested against the Roman Catholic Church and who set up their own church.

GLOSSARY

Provinces
Rural areas away from the capital and other large cities.

Radical
People who campaign for sweeping changes in politics and society. The word 'radical' comes from the Latin for 'root'; radical revolutionaries wanted to 'uproot' the government and introduce something completely new.

Roman Catholic
Someone who followed medieval Christian beliefs, with the Pope as the Head of the Church.

Royalist
A supporter of the king and his policies.

Sacked
Destroyed by an army.

Salons
Drawing-rooms of large houses in France. The places where groups of politicians and their friends met to discuss current affairs and revolutionary ideas.

Sans-culottes
Ordinary, working French men and women (and their supporters from other groups in society) who played an important part in revolutionary politics. Their views were radical.

Steward
Someone who looks after a house or lands for a lord or lady.

Stocks
A kind of public punishment in which the person sat with their feet held between two pieces of wood.

Taille personelle
A yearly tax on personal possessions, paid to the pre-revolutionary government in France.

Terrorist
Someone who uses violence – often against civilians – to fight for their political beliefs.

Tithe
A tax of one-tenth of produce, paid yearly to the Church.

Tranquillity
Peace.

Tribunal
A kind of court; the French revolutionary tribunals had power to sentence people to death.

Tyrant
A ruler who rules badly and unfairly.

Vestments
Special clothes worn during religious ceremonies.

Vingtième
A tax of one-twentieth of the value of land, paid yearly to the pre-revolutionary French government.

Glossary words in *italics* refer to the *French Revolution and Napoleon*.

INDEX

Page numbers in **bold** refer to sources/ captions

Acts of Union
　with Scotland 55
　with Wales 15
Alembert, Jean d' 70, 71
Alexander, Tsar of Russia **110**
American Declaration of
　Independence 51, **51**, 71
American Revolution 72, 77, 90
Anne, Queen 55, **55**
anti-Catholicism 33, 53, **57**, **58**
Aske, Robert 15
Austerlitz, battle of **106**, **107**

Banqueting House 34
Bastille **78**
beggars 30–31, **30**
Bible 10, 16, 19, 56
Blücher, Marshal 47
Boleyn, Anne 11, **11**, 12
Bonaparte *see* Napoleon
　Bonaparte
Bosworth, battle of 9
Bourbon dynasty 68
bourgeoisie **66–67**, 68, 71, 72
　post-Revolution 98, 118
　Third Estate **74–75**
　wealth of 77
Boxford church **16**, **18**, **19**
Boyne, battle of the 58, **59**
Bradshaw, John 46, **47**
Brissot, Jacques-Pierre **88–90**
Buckingham, George Villiers,
　Duke of 35–37, **35**
Burke, Edmund 88
Bury St Edmunds 14

café society **71**, 90
Calonne, Charles-Alexandre de 73
Campion, Edmund 19
Catherine of Aragon 11, **11**, 12
cavaliers 44
Charles I **32**, **36**, 36–47, **38**, **43**, **46**, 84, **85**
Charles II 49, 52, **52**, 53
Charles V, Emperor 11
Charles X, King of France 119
Church, in France 67, 81, **97**, 98, 102
Civil War, English 42–45
clergy, in France 71, **75**, **78**, **92**
　First Estate 74
　pre-Revolution **66**, 67
clothing **65**, **66**, **86**
Code Napoleon **102**, 103
Committee of Public Safety 92–94
Continental System 109, 110
Corday, Charlotte 91

Cranmer, Thomas 12, 16–18
Cromwell, Oliver 45, 46, **48**, 48–49, 52, 58, **114–115**
Cromwell, Richard 49
Cromwell, Thomas 12, **12**, 13, 14, 15
customs duties 40, **40**
Danton, Georges-Jacques **83**, **91**, 92, 93
David, Jacques-Louis **100**, **104**
Declaration of the Rights of Man
　and the Citizen **79**, 80, 87
Devon Prayer Book rebellion 17, **17**
Diderot, Denis 70, 71
Diggers 49, 51
Directory, the 94, **95**, 101
Dissolution of the Monasteries
　13–14, 21, 36
Divine Right of Kings 34–36, **68**, 70
Drake, Francis 19

economy, in France **72–74**, **97**
education, in France **97**
Edward VI 16, **18**
Eiffel Tower 118, **119**
Elizabeth I **18**, 19, **22**
enclosures 30–31
Estates-General 61, 68, 74–75, **76**, **77**, 84
Europe, wars in 100–101, 104–112

factories, in France 72
Fairfax, Sir Thomas 46
farming 26–27, 29, 30, **31**, 65, 98
Fawkes, Guy 33
feudalism 65, 74, 79, 98
Field of the Cloth of Gold 9, **9**
Flodden, battle of 10
Foxe's *Book of Martyrs* 19, **19**
Francis I 8, 9
Francis II, Emperor of Austria **88**
Franklin, Benjamin 70

Garibaldi 120
Girondins 90, **91**, 92
Glastonbury Abbey 13
Glorious Revolution 53, 54
guillotine **92**, 94
Gunpowder Plot 33, **33**

Haiti **89**
Hampden, John 40, **40**
Hanover 55
Hardwick, Bess of 28, **28**
Hardwick Hall 28, **28**
Hearne, Thomas 27
Henry VII 9, 15
Henry VIII 8–12, 15, 16, **18**
Hoare, Henry 60, **60**

houses 20, 21, 24–28
Hyde, Edward, Earl of Clarendon 43, 44

industrial revolution 4, **5**
inns 24, **24**
inventories 25, **27**
Ireland 42, 56–59

Jacobins 90, 91, 92, **93**, 94 100
James I 32, **32**, 33–36
James II **52**, 53, 58
Josephine, Empress 100, 101
jousting 8
Justices of the Peace (JPs) 15, 23

Lafayette, Marquis de 81, 90
Laud, William 41, **41**, 42
Lee, Rowland 15
Legislative Assembly **91**
Lenin, Vladimir Ilyich **121**
Levellers 49, **50**, 51
Locke, John 70
London, life in 24
Louis XIV, King of France **39**, 61, 68
Louis XV, King of France 68, 69
Louis XVI, King of France 68, 69, 71–72, **73**, 74, 76–77
　Divine Right belief **68**
　escape bid **82**, **89**
　execution **83**, **85**, 87
　retitled 80
Louis XVIII, King of France 113, **117–118**
Louis-Philippe, King of France 119
L'Ouverture, Toussaint **89**
Luther, Martin 10

Marat, Jean-Paul **91**
Marie-Antoinette, Queen of
　France **69**, 77, **82**, 88
Marie-Louise, Empress 104, **105**
Marritt, William 24, 25, **25**
Marseillaise, La 88, **89**, 118, **119**
Marston Moor, battle of 45
Marvell, Andrew 47
Mary I 1, 18, **18**
Mary II 53–55
Mary Rose 10
medicine 29
merchants 24–25
Méricourt, Théroigne de **86**, 87
Metternich, Prince **117**
Mirabeau, Comte de **75**, 80, 90
mob rule **78**, **82–83**, 90
monasteries 13, **13**, 14
money 22, 27
monks 13, 14

126

INDEX

Montacute House 20–21, **20**
Montesquieu, Charles, Baron de **71**
More, Sir Thomas 8, 12, **12**
Morgan, William 19
Mulcheney Abbey 13, **13**, 14

Napoleon Bonaparte **94**, 95, 96–116, 117, 118, 119
   exile **112–113**, **116**, 118
   rebuilding of France 102–103
   rise to power **96**, 99, **100–101**
   wars in Europe 100–101, **104–112**
National Assembly 75, 79–80, **89**
Navy 10, 44
Necker, Jacques 72, **73**
Nelson, Admiral Lord **108**
New Model Army 45–46, 48–49
new monarchy 8, 9
Newton, Sir Isaac 70
nobles **66**, 67, 78
   killed in revolution 92
   post-Revolution **98**
   Second Estate **74**
   social reform of 71–72

Paine, Tom **75**, **82**, **95**
Paris 79
   Caveau Café **71**
   Cordeliers Church **80**
   guillotine **92**, 94
   at the end of the Revolution 94
   sans-culottes **86**, 87, 90
   Tuileries 82, **83**
Parliament 12, 15, 35, 37–45, **42**, 49–55, **55**
peasants **64–65**, 73, 77, **92**
   feudalism 79, 87
   post-Revolution **98–99**
Peter the Great, Tsar of Russia 70

Pilgrim Fathers 35
Pilgrimage of Grace 15, **15**
plantations 56–57, **57**
Poor Law, 1601 31
porcelain **73**
poverty 27–31, 64, 65, 77, 79
puritans 19, 35, **37**, 41, **41**, 45, 52
Pym, John 37, **37**, 41–43, 44

Quakers 50, 52, 54, **54**

religion
   Catholicism 11, 14, **14**, 18, 19, 33, 37, 53, 54, 58–59
   Protestantism 10, 16, 17, **17**, 18, 19, 41, 58–59
republic 83, 86
revolutions 4–5, 84, 120–122
Revolutionary Calendar **93**, 96, 103
Revolutionary Tribunal **91**
Richard III 9
Richelieu, Cardinal 39, **39**
Rivoli, battle of **94**, **95**
Robespierre, Maximilien 75, **91–92**, 94, **101**
Roland, Manon **88**, **90**
roundheads 44
Rousseau, Jean-Jacques **71**
royal finances 13, 36–37, 40, 54
Rupert, Prince 44
Russia **110–111**
Russian Revolution 4, 121

Saint-Just, Louis-Antoine de **77**, **83**
salons 90
sans-culottes **86–87**, 90
science 70–71
Scotland 10, 33, 35, 41, 45, 55
ship money 40, 42
Sieyès, Canon 90

slavery 89, **90**
Solway Moss, battle of 10
Spain 19, 30, 40, 56
Spenser, Edmund 56, **56**
Stourhead House 60, **60**
Strafford, Earl of 42, **42**

taxes **65**, **73**, **74**, 77, 78, 79, 98
Tennis Court Oath **75**, 76
Third Estate **74**, 75, 76, **78**
Tichborne, Sir Henry 23, **23**
trade 24, 55, **72**, **97**
Trafalgar, battle of **108**
Tuileries, Paris 82, **83**

Valor Ecclesiasticus 13, **13**
Verney, Sir Edmund 43, 45
Verney, Sir Ralph 43
Versailles, Palace of 61, **61**, **68–69**, 76, **77**, 79
Vienna, Congress of **116–117**, 120
Voltaire 71

Wales 15, 19, 23, 26
wars 72, 88
   citizen army **99**
   Directory policy 94
   Napoleonic 100–101, 104–111, 118
Waterloo, battle of **113**
Wellington, Duke of **105**, **109**, **113**
Welsh surnames 15
William III 53, **53**, 54, 55, 58–59, **59**
Wolsey, Cardinal Thomas 10, 11
women 28–29, 65, **72**, **79**, **86–87**, 91, 99, **103**
Wordsworth, William 77
Wyclif, John 18

yeoman 26

ACKNOWLEDGEMENTS

Every effort has been made to contact the holders of copyright material but if any have been inadvertently overlooked the publishers will be pleased to make the necessary arrangements at the first opportunity.

Photographs The publishers would like to thank the following for permission to reproduce photographs on these pages:

T = top, B = bottom, C = centre, L = left, R = right

Ancient Art and Architecture Collection 17, 40, 122L; Barnaby's Picture Library 4L; Bibliothèque Nationale, Paris 103T; Bowes Museum, Barnard Castle, County Durham 83R; The Bridgeman Art Library 3L, 11L, 12T and B, 23, 34R, 35, 38C and B, 51C, 52T, 115L; The Bridgeman Art Library/Lauros-Giraudon 3R, 65B, 66R, 68T and B, 69C, 70BL, 79T and B, 81T, 83L, 85R, 86R, 89TL, 91TL and R, 92R, 95B, 96, 99, 100L and R, 101T, 102T, 104, 105T and BL, 108CL, 112T, 113T, 114, 116, 117B, 118R, 122R; The Bridgeman Art Library/Victoria and Albert Museum 113B; The Bridgeman Art Library/Yale University Art Gallery, New Haven 71B; The British Library 57B; Bulloz/Musée Carnavalet 67B; Bulloz/Bibliothèque Nationale, Paris 101B, 102B, 105BR; Collections 33C; E.T. Archive 39L and R, 64R, 69T (Dulwich Picture Gallery), 74, 75, 78L and R, 81B, 85 L and R, 91B, 92L, 110L, 111R; English Heritage 13L; Mary Evans Picture Library 5C, 70TR and CR; Fotomas Index 73L, 89B, 112B; Frick Collection, New York 10B; By gracious permission of Her Majesty the Queen 36, 37T, 53, 55; Robert Harding Picture Library 65T; Michael Holford 111L; The Hulton Deutsch Collection 27C, 29, 31T and B, 32B, 37B; The Hutchison Library/Tony Souter 117T; Impact Photos 26 (Pamla Toler), 103B (Eric Maulave/Cedri); Michael Jenner 24; A.F. Kersting 34L; Lauros-Giraudon 73R, 77, 88, 98T; Lauros-Giraudon/Musée de la Ville de Paris 86T, 87, 90, 93, 94B; The Mansell Collection 14, 19, 45, 48TR, 89TR, 94T, 95T, 120; Ampliaciones Reproducciones MAS, Barcelona 109C; By courtesy of the Director, National Army Museum, London 59T; The National Gallery, London 109T; National Galleries of Scotland 32C, 46; National Museum of Wales/Sudeley Castle 18; The National Portrait Gallery, London 11R, 33T, 48B, 52B; The National Trust 20, 21R, 28T and B, 60T and C; The Nelson Museum Monmouth 108CR; Musée d'Orange/ photo Bernard Delgado 72; Pacemaker 59C; © Photothèque des Musées Nationaux de la Ville de Paris by SPADEM 1995/Musée Carnavalet 67B (Debucourt, *Promenade au Palais Royal*) 71T (Anon, *Palais Royal, Caveau Café*), 80T (T. Demarchy, *Demolition of the Cordeliers Church*); Pepys Library, Magdalene College, Cambridge 10; Private Collection 22; Public Records Office, London 13R; © Photo Réunion des Musées Nationaux, Paris 66L (J.B Charpentier, *The Family of the Duke of Panthièvre*, 1768 Palace of Versailles), 97 (J. Vernet, *The Port of Bordeaux*, Musée de la Marine), 114 (J.B. Isabey, *The Congress of Vienna*, 1815 Musée du Louvre); Rex Features, London 48TL and TC; Steve Richards 30T; Royal Armouries, London 8, 9, 44; Sony UK 5L; South Somerset County District Council, Environment Department 21L, 54; Frank Spooner Pictures 4R, 5T and BR; Syndication International 51T; Victoria and Albert Museum, London 27T; Weidenfeld and Nicolson Archives 42, 108B; Zefa Picture Library 61.

Cover photographs The Bridgeman Art Library.

The authors and publishers gratefully acknowledge the following publications from which written sources in this book are drawn:

Oxford University Press for extracts from William Doyle, *The Oxford History of the French Revolution*, 1989; Blackwell Publishers Ltd for extracts from J.M. Thompson, *English Eye Witnesses*; Penguin Books Ltd for extracts from Alfred Cobban *The History of Modern France, Volumes I and II*, J.M. and M.J. Cohen, *Penguin Dictionary of Quotations*, 1960 and C. MacEvedy *Penguin Atlas of Modern History*; HarperCollins for extracts from Peter Vanstittart, *Voices of the Revolution*, 1989.

© HarperCollins *Publishers* 1995

Christopher Culpin and Fiona Macdonald assert the moral right to be identified as the authors of this work.

All rights reserved. No part of this publication may be reproduced, stored in a retrieval system, or transmitted in any form or by any means, electronic, mechanical, photocopying, recording or otherwise without the prior permission of the publisher.

First published in 1995 by Collins Educational
An imprint of Harper Collins *Publishers*
77–85 Fulham Palace Road
Hammersmith
London W6 8JB

ISBN 000 327281 8

Series planned by Nicole Lagneau
Edited by Helen Mortimer
Cover designed by Glynis Edwards
Book designed by Glynis Edwards and Derek Lee
Picture Research by Donna Thynne
Artwork by Julia Osorno, Linda Rogers Associates/Peter Dennis
Production by Mandy Inness
Printed and bound by Rotolito Lombarda, Italy